BE
ONE

FINDING CHRISTLIKE UNITY
IN A FRACTURED WORLD

Other Works by the Authors:

Choose to Learn:
Teaching for Success Every Day
by Russell T. and Lola S. Osguthorpe

Filled with His Love:
Strengthening Our Attachment to God and to Others
by Russell T. Osguthorpe

The Education of the Heart:
Rediscovering the Spiritual Roots of Learning
by Russell T. Osguthorpe

Forgotten Saints:
A Pioneer Story of Those Who Lived and Died Without a Trace
by Russell T. Osguthorpe

Pumpy and Poofy
Live it Up the Lord's Way
by Russell T. Osguthorpe

Podcast—Filled with His Love:
A podcast focused on strengthening attachment relationships
by Russell T. Osguthorpe

BE ONE

FINDING CHRISTLIKE UNITY IN A FRACTURED WORLD

RUSSELL T. OSGUTHORPE

LOLA S. OSGUTHORPE

CFI
An imprint of Cedar Fort, Inc.
Springville, Utah

Paperback ISBN 13: 978-1-4621-4741-0
eBook ISBN 13: 978-1-4621-4785-4

Published by CFI, an imprint of Cedar Fort, Inc.
2373 W. 700 S., STE 100, Springville, UT 84663
Distributed by Cedar Fort, Inc., www.cedarfort.com

  Library of Congress Cataloging Number: 2024931630

Cover design by Shawnda Craig
Cover design © 2022 Cedar Fort, Inc.
Edited and Typeset by Kayla Hofeling

Printed in the United States of America

10 9 8 7 6 5 4 3 2 1

Printed on acid-free paper

To our posterity, who bring us the joy of oneness everyday.

CONTENTS

PREFACE

THE PAIN WAS GETTING WORSE. I WASN'T SURE IF I NEEDED TO GO TO the hospital or if it might improve in time, but time didn't help. It continued to become more acute and harder to bear. My wife drove me to the emergency room; I checked in and got my needed help. The pain came from an infection that would not go away. I lay in bed waiting for the medication to work its magic, but the magic was not coming. As discouragement began to set in, Lolly knocked on the bedroom door and said, "You've got a visitor." At first, I thought, "I'm in no shape for visitors right now." But she knew that this visitor would be welcome. "It's Elder Soares," she announced.

Elder Ulisses Soares, a General Authority Seventy at the time, was on assignment in Bismarck, North Dakota, where my wife and I served as temple president and matron. When he learned I was recovering from an illness, he came to our home to see how I was doing. He moved a chair close to my bed, I sat down, and he and his traveling companion gave me a blessing. Even writing about the experience now, I can feel the love that came through his words as he pronounced the blessing. His expressions in the blessing, his hands, and his voice helped me feel God's love.

In the conclusion of his book *Compassion: the Great Healer's Art*, Elder Soares explains how we can all show God's love to others:

> Our beloved Savior invites us to be His hands in helping, serving, and succoring those in need. He invites us to be His feet so we might run to those who need our help and service. He invites us to be His eyes so we might always seek opportunities to serve. He invites us to be His ears to listen for those who might be crying out

for help. In all His compassion and mercy, He acted on behalf of those looking for physical, spiritual, and emotional healing.[01]

I needed physical, spiritual, and emotional healing on the day he came to give me a blessing. When our bodies are not well, our spirits and emotions also suffer. So when he blessed me, I felt lifted in all those ways. His ears heard about my need, his feet brought him to my bedroom, and his hands were laid upon my head in the same way the Savior laid His hands on His disciples when He was here on the earth.

My imagination allows me to experience Elder Soares's blessing anew as I write this preface. As I see that scene in my mind again, I can feel his compassion and the compassion of the Savior. In this book my wife, Lolly, and I show how compassion and imagination can lead us to a happier place where relationships flourish and where we grow toward oneness and Christlike unity. Such unity will help to overcome the turmoil, intolerance, and strife of a fractured world.

01. Ulisses S. Soares, *Compassion: The Great Healer's Art* (Salt Lake City: Deseret Book Company, 2023), p.130.

INTRODUCTION

"We ought to have the building up of Zion as our greatest object."
—*Joseph Smith*[02]

LAST YEAR, MY WIFE AND I STOOD WITH OUR FIVE CHILDREN AND THEIR spouses in the room where scholars believe Jesus might have administered and passed the sacrament to His disciples. The room was about the size of a Relief Society room, but the walls and ceiling were stone and plaster. We tried to imagine the scene of the Last Supper. We said very little. All we wanted to do was soak in the magnitude of what had happened in that small room. Then one of the children suggested that we sing "Abide with Me." This hymn has been a favorite of our family, so all of us began to sing. The acoustics expanded the sound beyond our voices, and for those few moments, we felt close to each other and very near to the Savior.

Following the Last Supper, Jesus and his disciples went to the Garden of Gethsemane, where Jesus would offer his last prayer on earth. He knew He was approaching the end and would be crucified. He knew His work was finished on the earth, so He knelt to offer an intercessory prayer. What is an intercessory prayer? It's a plea from the one praying on behalf of others, interceding for them. He was praying for His disciples who were with Him. But He was also praying and pleading with the Father for us. And what was His plea? What was his most powerful desire for us? That we might be one, as He and His Father are one.

---

02. *Teachings of the Presidents of the Church: Joseph Smith* (Salt Lake City: The Church of Jesus Christ of Latter-day Saints, 2007), 186.

Oneness: that was Christ's deepest desire. And because the Restoration has revealed to the world the true nature of God, we know what oneness means. Jesus and his Father are separate beings, but one in purpose and mission. They both want the same things for all of us, their children. Jesus might have prayed that we would all live with Him and His Father one day in the coming life, but He knew that the only way for us to be with Them in the eternities was to become one with Them and each other in mortality: "That they may be one, even as we are one: I in them, and thou in me, that they may be made perfect in one" (John 17:22–23).

We sometimes worry about our righteousness. "Am I keeping the commandments as well as I should? Am I keeping the covenants I've made with God?" This is an individualistic approach to the gospel—a focus on oneself. But as President Russell M. Nelson has taught, "Salvation is an individual matter; exaltation is a family matter."[03] We like to think of family in the broadest sense possible. Yes, we focus first on the relationships we foster in our own homes, but we are all brothers and sisters, and in Christ's final prayer, He was praying, "That they *all* may be one; as thou, Father, art in me, and I in thee" (John 17:21; emphasis added). We gain exaltation as united families, but we establish Zion by becoming united with all our brothers and sisters. The whole city of Enoch was of "one heart and one mind" (Moses 7:18). In 4 Nephi, the people "were in one, the children of Christ, and heirs to the kingdom of God" (4 Nephi 1:17).

If being one with God and with others is the highest aim of mortality, what is the adversary's greatest goal? Evil takes many forms, but all those forms eventually lead to separation and division. The adversary's first goal is to break up families, to pit one family member against another. Approximately one in four adults in America is estranged from a family member.[04] But the forces of separation and division reach far beyond the family. Race, gender, religion, socioeconomic status, education, sexual orientation, disability, age—these can all be sources of social division. As a culture, we are not coming closer to oneness; we are moving farther away.

---

03. Russell M. Nelson, *Salvation and Exaltation*, General Conference, The Church of Jesus Christ of Latter-day Saints, Apr. 2008, Gospel Library App.

04. Karl Pillemer, *Fault Lines: Fractured Families and How to Mend Them*, (New York City: Avery, 2020), p.4.

If God's highest purpose is to teach us to "love one another; as I have loved you" (John 13:34), then the adversary's highest purpose is to teach us to hate one another as he has hated us. The word *love* conjures up all kinds of positive emotions. We all want to love and be loved. And the word *hate* sickens us. It is a powerful negative emotion. Hate is so negative because it can become a source of one's identity. Think of the Lamanites in the Book of Mormon. They hated the Nephites for centuries. Hate was one of their defining characteristics, leading to constant conflict and war with their enemies, the Nephites. Today, people might identify as liberals or conservatives, and that one characteristic can cause them to treat each other as enemies. White supremacists hate Blacks, Jews, Asians, and Muslims and treat them as enemies. Homophobic people hate LGBTQ+ people and treat them with hostility. Fundamentalists of any religion can bring hatred toward any group, such as women, pro- or anti-abortionists, and those with disabilities.

We might wish that the powers of divisiveness and intolerance would go away. We might even deny the increasing frequency of intolerance in our society because it is so unpleasant to think about. But it's here. It's real. And it affects many people every day. To show how serious a problem we have with intolerance, consider these startling facts about American society: Hate crimes increased by nearly 12% from 2020 to 2021. That figure includes over 7,000 individual hate crimes in one year alone. Hate crimes arise because of offenders' biases. Nearly 65% of the victims of hate crimes in America are targeted because of the offender's bias toward race, ethnicity, or ancestry.[05] Sounds like we're right back to the Lamanites and Nephites, as if people are saying: "I'm a Lamanite, and you're a Nephite, so I hate you and want to kill you." This is what is happening today in our own country and throughout the world. "I'm White, and you're Black, so based on that one characteristic, I hate you and want to kill you." But other biases lead to hate crimes. Sexual orientation and religion are the next most common biases that lead to hate crimes in America. Nearly 16 percent of hate crimes are based on sexual orientation and almost as many (14 percent) on religion.[06] These are not pretty statistics, but they describe the seriousness of our current problem.

---

05. Washington, D.C. FBI National Press Office, 13 March 2023, https://www.fbi.gov/news/press-releases/fbi-releases-supplemental-2021-hate-crime-statistics.
06. Ibid.

Intolerance can lead to hate, and hate can lead to violence against others. The adversary is keeping score, and he is likely quite pleased with his campaign to conquer the positive forces of love.

Some might read these statistics and say, "Well, I know racism is a problem, but these numbers seem exaggerated; things are better than they used to be." In some ways, things might be better. We're not in the midst of a civil war with slavery hanging in the balance. But here's the problem: multiple polls have shown that Whites in America believe we as a nation are making much more progress than do Blacks. For example, only 37 percent of Whites say that our country hasn't gone far enough in giving equal rights to Blacks, while 78 percent of Blacks respond similarly. In other words, most Whites believe that Blacks and Whites have equal rights in America, while most Blacks believe we have a long way to go before they will be treated the same as Whites. Fully 45 percent of Americans believe that it has become more acceptable to express racist views in recent years; only 23 percent believe that expressing racist views has become less acceptable.[07]

Racism does not appear to be decreasing; in fact, it appears to be increasing. Again, the adversary seems to be doing quite well on this count. President Russell M. Nelson has condemned racism and racist violence:

> We join with many throughout this nation and around the world who are deeply saddened at recent evidences of racism and a blatant disregard for human life. We abhor the reality that some would deny others respect and the most basic of freedoms because of the color of his or her skin. We are also saddened when these assaults on human dignity lead to escalating violence and unrest.
>
> The creator of us all calls on each of us to abandon attitudes of prejudice against any group of God's children. Any of us who has prejudice toward another race needs to repent!
>
> During the Savior's earthly mission, He constantly ministered to those who were excluded, marginalized, judged, overlooked, abused, and discounted. As His followers, can we do anything less?

---

07. Pew Research Center, 9 April 2019, https://www.pewresearch.org/social-trends/2019/04/09/race-in-america-2019/.

The answer is no! We believe in freedom, kindness, and fairness for all of God's children![08]

IMAGINATION IS OUR LAST SANCTUARY

So, how do we conquer all the divisiveness in our world? Our answer to this question is that we must first imagine a different world, a world where hate can be turned into love—where we can be one. We need to envision images of Christlike unity. How can we reach a destination we have never imagined? Imagination is essential to any progress we hope to make. It has been said that imagination is our last sanctuary.[09] Each of us has the power to see a different world, a new world coming together where intolerance of others because of skin color, sexual orientation, or religious beliefs turns into understanding. And that means we need a special kind of imagination, what we are calling "compassionate imagi-nation." Imagination all by itself is neutral—it can lead to good or evil. After all, the one who commits a mass shooting often imagines the scene of carnage in his mind before he pulls the trigger. So, we need to qualify this act of cognition and emotion. We don't need any kind of imagina-tion; we need imagination founded on the teachings of Jesus Christ, a moral imagination full of compassion toward others.

08. Russell M. Nelson, "President Nelson Condemns Racism, Pleads for Peace," *Church News*, 1 June 2020, https://www.thechurchnews. com/2020/6/1/23265006/president-nelson-addresses-race-in-social-media-post.
09. *Night Train to Lisbon*, directed by Bille August (Studio Hamburg Filmproduktion, 2013).

CHAPTER 1
BECOMING ONE

A SINGLE WORD—A WORD WITH ONLY THREE LETTERS—CAN CONVEY such power, such meaning. It can bring an end to disagreements and misunderstandings. It can wash away resentment and revenge, lift a troubled heart, or mend a broken one. It can soften, heal, cheer, and gladden. This word can help us yield to God and each other, never to be separated again. The word is *one*.

When God's children become contentious, His counsel is clear: "Be one; and if ye are not one ye are not mine" (Doctrine & Covenants 38:27). Oneness is a divine quality. The Savior's relationship with His Father is the ultimate example of oneness. Lucifer's rebellion against God is the ultimate non-example—the stark opposite of what we seek. When Christ said, "Be one," He invited us to unite with Him and God the Father so we could experience the same divine oneness that defines deity. Only then can we develop Christlike unity with others.

Lolly: Our five children and their spouses had the privilege of visiting the Holy Land a few years ago. After attending church services in the BYU Jerusalem Center, we spent the afternoon in the Garden of Gethsemane. We had the area all to ourselves as we shared scriptures and spent private time as a family and couples. As we wove our path through the ancient olive grove, I imagined where Jesus might have suffered for us on that fateful night and where he might have knelt next to a gnarled olive tree. There is an unmistakable serenity that fills this beautiful valley next to Jerusalem. Protected and secluded from the noise and crowds of the city, we envisioned Him offering that great intercessory prayer before the cruel deeds of betrayal, judgment, and crucifixion took place.

During His final prayer, Christ was facing certain punishment and death, but not thinking of His pain or suffering. Rather, he was thinking of us—each one of us.

What did He pray for specifically? That we might become one with Him, His Father, and each other. The process of becoming one is the meaning of atonement—the quality of being at one with God and each other. He said, "That they all may be one; as thou, Father, art in me, and I in thee, that they also may be one in us: that the world may believe that thou hast sent me" (John 17:21).

Without the truths of the Restoration, without Joseph's First Vision, we could not understand the meaning of these words recorded in the book of John. In this greatest of all prayers, the Lord was teaching us that we could become one as the Father and Son and Holy Ghost are one—one in purpose, one in mission, one in desire, one in action. Think of it. What amazing words! The Lord was helping us see that even though God the Father and His Son Jesus Christ are separate beings with bodies of flesh and bone, they can be one.

But then the Savior goes even further. He prays not only that we can be one with Him and His Father, but that we might become one with each other and feel the infinite love of the Father: "And the glory which thou gavest me I have given them; that they may be one, even as we are one: I in them, and thou in me, that they may be made perfect in one" (John 17:22–23).

Without the atonement, oneness would be impossible. Real oneness in a marriage, a family, or with friends—the kind of oneness that Christ prayed for in that great intercessory prayer—can come only when we accept His atonement. Because real oneness cannot come unless we feel God's love for us and all His children, here are the questions we might ask ourselves: How can we fulfill Christ's prayer? How can we become one with God the Father and His Son Jesus Christ? How can we become one with each other? If we do these things, we will partake fully of Christ's Atonement.

How can we become one with our spouse, children, and friends? When a commentator asked President Hinckley to name the Prophet Joseph Smith's greatest contribution, without hesitation, President Hinckley responded, "His greatest contribution I think is defining the nature of deity."[10] Knowing the true nature of the Godhead, understanding that they are three separate beings, but that they can still be one with each other, is the most important truth we comprehend because only when we know God and His Son Jesus Christ can we begin to build upon their example to become one with them and with others.

There is a powerful relationship between loving one another and experiencing the love of God. This part of Christ's prayer teaches us that God the Father loves us as much as He loves His only begotten Son—His beloved Son.

However, it's difficult to feel God's love if we are at odds with our spouse, with a brother or sister, or with a friend. The more we become one with each other, the more we can feel God's love, and the more we feel God's love, the more we can express that love to everyone around us. Oneness is all about love. It's about understanding one another so well that we come to love one another. This principle is easy to see in families. What is a dysfunctional family? A family at odds with one another. What is a healthy eternal family? A family where everyone's actions—husband to wife, parent to child, sibling to sibling—are motivated by love. In this way, love just keeps growing, and oneness increases.

Becoming one with God and with each other is a lifelong process. It has no beginning and no end. But the simple act of trying to be one, growing closer to God and others, changes us. We become more open to differing points of view. Our capacity to experience others' grief and joy expands. So we keep trying. We keep forgiving. We reason together in a spirit of seeking truth. We let go of the past and let the future fill us with hope. To become one with each other, we try to see things through their eyes instead of our own. We ask questions when we don't understand. We accept whatever the other person can offer without judging them.

The covenant path is a path that leads to oneness. Making and keeping covenants ties us to God and each other. Without covenants, we are cast adrift in a sea of turbulence, confusion, and self-centeredness.

---

10. Jon Meachem, "Solid, Strong, True," *Newsweek*, 16 October 2005, https://www.newsweek.com/solid-strong-true-121197.

In my own life, I want to respond to the prayer that Jesus uttered in the final moments of His life. I want to learn more about being one with Them, as He said, "I in them and thou in me." I want to learn more about how to be one with my family members and friends, as He prayed, "that all may be made perfect in one." I know I will be working on this my whole life. But I also know that the Savior came to earth for this express purpose—to help us learn how to become one, and I also know that He has the power through His love and grace to help us achieve oneness.

Lolly: I want to unlock the key to what oneness means for me through personal revelation. I believe that revelation is helped by temple worship and striving to keep my temple covenants. As I come to know God through my temple covenants, I feel Heaven opening a bit to my view and the love of God surrounding me in my efforts to know Him. Feelings of oneness surround me, and I can imagine what it was like before I came to earth. I have so much love for the Savior because of His sacrifice on my behalf. His example helps me daily as I seek to be one with Him and the Father. As I petition God daily in my prayers, I seek to know Him, to know His Son, and to develop oneness with them. Just as I develop a closeness with my spouse and other family members, I must seek their companionship as often as possible. As I strive to obey, sacrifice, and consecrate my daily activities to God, that oneness increases, and I feel Heaven's closeness.

Achieving oneness demands that we develop compassionate imagination. After all, oneness is an imaginary thought. We do not become the same being. Rather, we envision agreement, reconciliation, and understanding—a unity of desire and goals. Without imagination, a Christ-centered imagination, oneness would be impossible. With such imagination, we can "be one," and everything that God wants for us is made possible.

CHAPTER 2
COMPASSIONATE
IMAGINATION

IMAGINATION TOUCHES EVERY ASPECT OF HUMAN LIFE. WITHOUT IT, WE would have no paintings or sculptures by Michelangelo or Rodin, no poems or novels by Maya Angelou or Jane Austen, no music by Mozart or Bernstein, or dance by Anna Pavlova or Martha Graham. All art is an act of creation, and imagination is the fuel that powers such creation. But imagination is also the source of invention. Without it, we would have no cars, airplanes, or cell phones. The inventor must first imagine the object before designing and producing it. Without the capacity to imagine, we could not set goals for the future, plan, strategize, scheme, or dream. We must imagine the future before we can live it. Even the past relies on imagination. A past event must be reconstructed in our mind. Memory relies on our ability to reimagine it.

Even more important than the role of imagination in creativity or in memory is the power of imagination in human relations. On the grandest scale, for two warring countries to negotiate peace, the leaders must first imagine what a mutual accord will look like. To end their hostility, enemies must conceive a harmony that may have never existed between them. Likewise, a married couple at odds with each other must imagine what their relationship would be like if they stopped fighting and began to communicate with more understanding. More importantly, empathy itself demands imagination. One must imagine how another experiences pain or joy to experience that same emotion.

The point is that however broadly you have conceived the human quality of imagination, you will begin to see it even more broadly as you read this book. Imagination can pave a pathway to truth. Discoveries are based on one's ability to see what has not been seen before, to understand an old idea in a new way, and to sense the thrill of knowing something, really knowing it, for the first time. Most want to become more creative, inventive, and knowledgeable. Most would like to become more skilled at forming and nurturing human relationships. The key to all such endeavors, we believe, is to recognize the power of our imagination and the imagination of others to learn how to harness that power, draw upon it, and strengthen it.

As Albert Einstein once said, "Imagination is more important than knowledge. Knowledge is limited. Imagination encircles the world."[11] We live in an era that extols knowledge more than imagination. For example, the advent of artificial intelligence is an ironic twist on human values and abilities. The invention of ChatGPT required an impressive amount of imagination, but if students copies their whole essays from ChatGPT, they have not improved their creative capacity.

William James, one of the pioneers of American psychology, once said: "Unclamp your intellectual and practical machinery, and let it run free, and the service it will do you will be twice as good."[12] Because imagination is central to the definition of what it means to be human, philosophers, psychologists, neuroscientists, and religionists have been trying to understand it for millennia. The real irony is that the only way to comprehend the depth and breadth of being imaginative is to become more imaginative in the investigation itself. As James said, we need to unclamp our imaginations and let them "run free." But we can't let them run free in any direction, or we risk self-destruction. Like all human thought, imagination has moral implications because it leads to action—some moral, while others are not.

---

11. Albert Einstein and Annabel Acton, "10 Einstein Quotes to Fire Up Your Creativity," *Inc.*, 2021, https://www.inc.com/annabel-acton/10/einstein-quotes-to-fire-up-your-creativity.html.

12. Marvin C. Shaw, "Paradoxical Intention in the Life and Thought of William James," *American Journal of Theology & Philosophy* 7:5–16, January 1986, https://www.jstor.org/stable/27943676.

Because imagination has moral implications, I prefer the term compassionate imagination. What is compassionate imagination? There are various meanings for the term, but here's my definition:

> Compassionate imagination is a process that leads to oneness with God and unity with others. Thoughts may come in words, images, impressions, or feelings. These thoughts increase our faith and capacity to fulfill our purpose in mortality. Whether a thought comes from reason, observation, or the Holy Ghost, it will always lead us toward righteous action.

Think of the brother of Jared. He had to imagine barges that would carry his people across the ocean. He had to imagine them before he could build them, just as Nephi had to envision the ship before he built it. The Lord did not send a sheaf of blueprints. When the brother of Jared began to struggle with knowing how he would provide light inside the barges, again, the Lord did not send a three-dimensional model for him as a pattern. He asked the brother of Jared to bring back a proposal and exercise his imaginative power—to unclamp his brain and conceive of something he had never seen before. Such exercise of our imagination can bring us closer to the Lord. The brother of Jared was drawn so close that he saw the Lord's finger.

The Lord knew that the brother of Jared had good intentions. He wanted to provide light when the barges were submerged because he loved his people and knew that if they had to cross the ocean in total darkness, they might become so agitated and anxious that they could not bear it. So he used his imagination—compassionate imagination. Moses also had compassionate imagination; how else could he have envisioned freeing hundreds of thousands, maybe millions, of the children of Israel?

Lolly: Another historical figure was Marie Curie, a multidimensional woman with compassionate imagination when she used her initial discovery of radium to help wounded soldiers on the battlefield of World War I. Curie put her scientific research on hold, boxed up her radium, and hid it in a safety deposit vault at a local bank in Bordeaux during the war. By redirecting her efforts to saving lives, she invented a radiological car—a mobile x-ray unit called the "Little Curie" for the battlefield that saved hundreds of soldiers' lives. She trained over 150 women to operate the mobile units and had to figure out how to power them. Curie's "radiological car" was a vehicle containing an X-ray machine and photographic darkroom equipment—which could be driven right up to the battlefield where army surgeons could use X-rays to guide their surgeries.[13] She knew her invention could save lives, but did not have any vision of how many ways radiation is used to save lives today. However, her discovery also led to the development of the atomic bomb to end World War II. That is why we must use our God-given power of imagination in righteous ways.

The scriptures teach that we can "mount up in the imagination of [our] thoughts as upon eagles' wings" (Doctrine & Covenants 124:99). We also learn from sacred text that we must beware of vain imaginations (1 Nephi 12:18). Vain imaginations lead to selfishness. Compassionate imagination leads to righteous ends. Consider the imagery of how imagination inspired by the Lord can help us soar on "eagles' wings." The scriptural use of the phrase *eagles' wings* can mean many things. But in this case, it seems to refer to how the Lord's limitless power can help us imagine and act on thoughts that can lead us to exaltation.

The goal in this book is to help us examine our imaginative powers so that we can use those powers to build Zion. We covenant in the temple to establish Zion, but what does that mean? When we do missionary work or perform proxy ordinances for the dead, we contribute to the gathering, but establishing Zion is an additional step beyond the gathering. It's about becoming one with God and with each other. I am convinced that Enoch and his followers had to conceive Zion before they built it. They had to imagine their way from intolerance to tolerance, love, and oneness. There is no better example in the scriptures of real oneness than the city of Enoch. Their efforts in striving to live the celestial law were so strong that they began living the law, and so they were lifted up to heaven.

There were no poor among those who lived in the city of Enoch because they had compassion for one another. They left no one out. They never wrote off a brother or sister as being beyond help. When help was needed, they gave it. They imagined a world without strife, and they created it. We have a hard time imagining how intolerance could be

---

13. Eve Curie, *Madame Curie: A Biography*, (New York City: Doubleday, 1939).

abolished in our current world. But how could we ever create such a world if we cannot imagine it?

Compassionate imagination helps us see the world not as it is but as it might become. And by the world, I mean our microcosm, however small that might be. Our world is our family, our neighborhood, our ward, etc. Peace would reign everywhere if everyone had peace within their home and neighborhood. That is one of the messages of the Book of Mormon: that it takes only two people to create conflict, and the conflict between two people can expand metastatically until the cancer of hate destroys everyone in its grasp. Zion will never be established until we learn how to imagine a world where compassion cures all social ills that affect us.

The HEART Approach to Becoming One

If we examine how those in the past have developed oneness, we see that they all used the same approach. As President Nelson has taught, they repented daily. The natural man and woman within each of us is a powerful force, so we live daily in repentance. As those in the city of Enoch overcame the temptations of the flesh, they gradually became of "one heart." I believe the word *heart* can help us today to become one. In the context of this book, *heart* connotes both spirit and body—the whole soul. Our obedience must be whole-souled, or we will not become one with God or each other. So, we offer the word *heart* as an acronym for the type of repentance that will lead us to oneness, the type of repentance needed to expand our compassionate imagination.

In the HEART approach, the *H* stands for Hear Him, the *E* for Envision Oneness and Christlike Unity, the *A* for Act in Faith, the *R* for Recognize the Hand of God, and the *T* for Thank the Lord for His Blessings. These are the ways to increase our compassionate imagination so that we can become one with God and feel Christlike unity with others. I believe we will gradually become one if we think of the word *heart* and the meaning behind the individual letters we have suggested. The scriptures use the phrase "one heart" often. The most well-known is the description of those who lived in the city of Enoch: "And the Lord called his people Zion, because they were of *one heart* and one mind, and dwelt in righteousness, and there was no poor among them" (Moses 7:18; emphasis added). The following scriptural occurrences of the term *one heart* are also powerful reminders of how important this concept is: "And

I will give them *one heart*, and I will put a new spirit within you" (Ezekiel 11:19; emphasis added), "And the multitude of them that believed were of *one heart* and of one soul" (Acts 4:32; emphasis added), "They shall be my people, and I will be their God: and I will give them *one heart*, and one way" (Jeremiah 32:38–39; emphasis added), "Be determined in one mind and in *one heart*, united in all things" (2 Nephi 1:21; emphasis added).

The word *heart* refers to the innermost center of the person. When we say "wholehearted" or "whole-souled," we refer to the person's innermost desires and hopes—the whole person. Sometimes, the word *soul* is synonymous with *spirit*. But at times, the word *soul* is referred to as the spirit and body combined: "And the spirit and the body are the soul of man. And the resurrection from the dead is the redemption of the soul" (Doctrine and Covenants 88:15–16). Likewise, the word *heart* can also refer to the combination of the body and the spirit—the whole person. We imagine with our mind or spirit; we act with our body. So, in mortality, our body and spirit are united and cannot be separated. We like to think of the heart as the uniting force of the body with the spirit. When the heart stops, the spirit ascends to the spirit world, and the body descends to the grave.

To be compassionate in mortality, we must use our bodies. We must act, and action demands physical energy. We may have a deep-felt desire to help an aging parent struggle through the final years of life, but what if we don't feel we have the energy to give the needed care? Our compassionate service will not be wholehearted. We heard a woman recently express her dismay that she was full of desire to help her father deal with a terminal illness, but she had just helped her mother through a similar ordeal, and she feared she couldn't do it all over again. She feared that her heart would not be in it. She wanted her compassion to be wholehearted, whole-souled.

Compassionate imagination is all about action. It leads to action, and that action can lead to more compassionate imagination. If we put our whole heart into something, the Lord will reveal how we can meet life's demands. Trials and challenges can be overcome, but we must imagine our way through them in a wholehearted way and know deep down that by the Lord's grace, we will succeed.

THE HEART APPROACH—H: HEAR HIM

WHEN PRESIDENT NELSON ASKED US TO RECEIVE MORE PERSONAL REV-elation, he used the words God the Father spoke as He introduced the Savior to the young prophet Joseph in the Sacred Grove: "Hear Him!" These two powerful words can help anyone wanting more personal revelation. Sometimes, however, one might expect the revelatory experience to be mystical, something one can rarely experience. President Nelson wants us to receive personal revelation often, and he knows that such divine communication can come to us if we open ourselves to it.

Elder Dale G. Renlund of the Quorum of the Twelve has taught how reason, observation, faith, and revelation relate. In many ways, he has helped broaden the definition of revelation. Here are his words: "When we start with an inclination to believe, observation leads to faith. As faith grows, reason facilitates the transformation of faith into revelatory knowledge, and revelatory knowledge produces added faith."[14]

Faith is a principle of action—so Elder Renlund says that when we allow ourselves to believe in the Savior and His mission, we will begin to see evidence of His glory all around us. When we observe all these things, our faith will grow. As our faith grows, the Lord will inspire us in ways we had never expected, and as that inspiration increases, so will our faith.

So many wonder if they are receiving divine inspiration or if the thoughts that come to them are their own thoughts. Mormon taught us that if it leads to good, that's the test; it comes from God. President

---

14. Dale G. Renlund, *Reason, Observation, Faith and Revelation*, devotional address at Brigham Young University, 22 August 2023, https://speeches.byu.edu/talks/dale-g-renlund/observation-reason-faith-and-revelation/.

Hinckley also taught this principle, and Elder Renlund expresses it wonderfully:

> Personal revelation is facilitated by understating and formulating questions from multiple angles. Formulation and reframing questions require observation, reason, and faith. At one time or another, many of us have asked ourselves, "How do I know whether the thought I have is my own or if it is from the Holy Ghost?" This is a reasonable question. Perhaps a better question, and certainly a more actionable one, is this: "Should I act on this particular thought?" . . .
>
> These are the criteria to determine whether we should act on a particular thought: the thought promotes believing in Heavenly Father and Jesus Christ; it promotes loving and serving Them; and it promotes doing good. If the thought meets these criteria, does it really matter whether it was planted directly by the Holy Ghost in that exact moment or if the thought arose thanks to a lifetime of experiences and prior decisions? In reality, it doesn't. But observation and reason provide a filter through which we determine whether to act on an impression.[15]

In the context of this book, we might ask ourselves, "Did I imagine that thought, or did it come from the Holy Ghost?" If our thought meets the criteria Elder Renlund offered, it doesn't really matter. Does the thought promote a belief in Heavenly Father and Jesus Christ? Does it promote loving and serving Them? Does it promote doing good? If our thought meets these requirements, we don't need to worry about the source of the thought. The thought might have come from a book we were reading, a conversation we had with a friend, a painting we saw in a museum—it doesn't really matter. The thing that matters is where the thought leads us. If it leads us closer to God and His children, to a feeling of oneness and Christlike unity, then it doesn't matter where our thought or impression came from.

This approach to personal revelation is somewhat freeing. We don't need to experience some unexplainable, mystical connection with God; we simply need to be open to what God wants us to do and then let our compassionate imagination lead us to a good action. Elder Renlund's criteria fits perfectly with my definition of compassionate imagination. This

---

15. Ibid.

means we must find ways to free our imagination to unclamp our brains. We need to give up rigid ways of thinking—old, worn-out strategies that no longer work—and open ourselves to the soul-stirring knowledge that God wants us to receive. Because the Lord is all-knowing, He has no shortage of truths to teach us; He is never reluctant to inspire the one who is ready to receive, so we need to let ourselves be ready to hear Him.

Chapter 3
Accept the Deliverer

When we exercise our compassionate imagination, we can hear the Lord's promptings to change. He can help us imagine the change we must make to draw closer to Him and our loved ones. As we heed those promptings, we can also hear Him as He helps us feel forgiveness just as Enos did when he knelt to pray and heard the Lord say, "Thy sins are forgiven thee, and thou shalt be blessed" (Enos 1:5).

Elder David A. Bednar has taught that we need to embrace change. We need to be open to how God wants us to change. If we are to become one with God, we need to listen to His promptings and follow them:

> We are to come unto the Savior, we are to follow Him, and we are to be born again. We are to experience the mighty change of heart. Repentance is change. Learning and education [produce] change. The essence of our mortal experience is to not remain the same. Oftentimes people will say, "Ah, just leave me alone. I like things the way things are." Well, God doesn't like things the way they are in us. I'm not saying that in a negative way. It's not that He's unhappy, but we are not here in this mortal existence to just stay the same. So, we are blessed with remarkable spiritual gifts. The restoration of the Gospel teaches us our eternal purpose and destiny, and you don't achieve that destiny by just hunkering down and staying the same. The natural man and the natural woman [hate] change. The man and woman of Christ [learn] to love change and the lessons that are learned in the process. So, I think one of the fundamental

aspects of overcoming the natural man and the natural woman is not resisting change, but embracing change and learning from it.[16]

Personal change means we need to imagine a new way of acting, a new way of being. Change is not instant. A change of heart takes time. And during change, we need to be compassionate toward ourselves. Repentance itself is a process that demands compassionate imagination.

Consider the most far-reaching change in human history: the Savior's resurrection. In that singular moment, He delivered us from the finality of physical death and the mental and emotional torment of spiritual death. These two conditions held us captive before Easter morning, but following His resurrection, we were held captive no longer. We knew that we would live again after mortality and that we could repent and be forgiven of any sin, mistake, or unkind act we had ever committed.

He is our deliverer. He is the one who frees us. What change could be more powerful than this? And who would resist this change? Who would say, "Well, I liked it better the old way—I don't want to live forever." Or, "I don't need the forgiveness, comfort, or strength Christ offers me." He changed the world when He was resurrected. But He also changed us, as it says in Alma:

> Behold, he changed their hearts; yea, he awakened them out of a deep sleep, and they awoke unto God. Behold, they were in the midst of darkness; nevertheless, their souls were illuminated by the light of the everlasting word. . . . and their souls did expand, and they did sing redeeming love. And I say unto you that they are saved (Alma 5:7–9).

He is our deliverer. He frees us from the captivity of physical death and releases us from the bondage of sin. Captivity is an awful thing. I once visited the Utah State Prison, and on the way to my car, I looked back at that dismal fortress of bars and concrete. Even today, the images that stick with me are the arms of several prisoners hanging out of the barred windows—if we can call them windows. It was as if they were looking at me and pleading with me: "Take me with you. Please take me with you." They wanted to be released from captivity. But of course, I was powerless to do anything to end their stay behind those bars.

---

16. David A. Bednar, *Living in Revelation*, 31 January 2023, a talk given at Ensign College, https://www.ensign.edu/devotional/elder-david-a-bednar-and-jeff-simpson-01-2023.

Christ is the only one who can deliver us from the cords of sin that hold us captive. But what is our part in this deliverance? We need to do nothing to be resurrected. But what about our part in deliverance from sin?

In the third chapter of 3 Nephi, Lachoneus, king of the Nephites, knew that the Gadianton robbers were coming to slaughter his people, so what did he do? He built fortifications around the city, created a military structure, and told the people they needed to repent if they wanted the Lord's help. Deliverance comes because we give the Lord something to work with—our faith, our effort, our righteousness. The children of Israel were delivered from the slavery the Egyptians had forced upon them, but it took them 40 more years in the wilderness to be delivered from the bondage of sin. We play a part in our own deliverance.

As Elder Bednar said, we need to embrace change—especially the change we need to make in ourselves. When Alma the Younger experienced a divine visitation, he turned away from his former self and put on a new self. He stopped criticizing the Church. His former self was the naysayer. The detractor. The cynic. The one who tried to draw people away from the Church. But he not only stopped all those negative behaviors—he put on a totally new self. He became one of the most effective missionaries the Church had ever known. The Savior delivered him. He was forgiven of his sins. But consider what he did as part of that deliverance. He devoted himself to helping others make the change that he had experienced in himself. He was truly born again and wanted others to be born again.

If we are to embrace change, we need first to imagine the change. We also need to use our imagination to remember the images of deliverance that the children of Israel experienced. Imagination leads us forward, but it also goes backward in time. The prophets constantly reminded the children of Israel in the Bible and the people of Lehi in the Book of Mormon to remember how their ancestors had been delivered, because the image of deliverance can give us hope that we too can be delivered. Compassion is also a present action and an action of the past. Reflection on the feelings of deliverance we experienced in the past can help us embrace change in the present. The more we can imagine being delivered, the greater our power to change will be.

CHAPTER 4

SET YOUR FACE
LIKE A FLINT

IF WE WANT TO HEAR HIM, WE NEED TO OBEY HIM. THE MORE WE OBEY His word, the more His words inspire us to use our compassionate imagination to do His work. And sometimes understanding sacred text is challenging. I think most would agree that we need a well-developed sense of imagination to understand some of the words of Isaiah. Isaiah 50 is no exception. But Jacob saw this chapter as applying to his people, and I'm certain Mormon also knew it would apply to us today. One reason Isaiah's metaphors are challenging is because he says in a few words what many writers take paragraphs to explain. That's because Isaiah is what we might call a poet-prophet, and poets say things in the fewest words possible.

As Lolly and I reread chapter seven of 2 Nephi in our morning study, we found his metaphors compelling. Let's begin with the first verse of this chapter, quoting Isaiah: "Yea, for thus saith the Lord: Have I put thee away, or have I cast thee off forever? For thus saith the Lord: Where is the bill of your mother's divorcement?" Here, Isaiah is comparing his relationship with the children of Israel to a marriage between a man and a woman, and he's asking, "Did I divorce you? No, I did not."

Now, on to the next line in the verse: "To whom have I put thee away, or to which of my creditors have I sold you?" In Old Testament times, if you could not pay your creditors, you could sell your family members to pay off your debt. But the Lord is saying, "Did I do that? Did I try to get rid of you? No, I did not."

Now, here's the clincher phrase in this verse: "Yea, to whom have I sold you? Behold, for your iniquities have ye sold yourselves, and for your transgressions is your mother put away." The Lord is trying to explain that he did not distance himself from them; *they* distanced themselves from *Him*. But the Lord loves us infinitely, and His mercy is never-ending, so even with our transgressions, we can still dwell with Him and His Father in the eternities. All we need to do is repent.

Elder Holland explains it this way:

> These children will yet have a happy home and sealed parents. In the last days, that bill of divorcement against their mother will be set aside, and so will the demands of any creditors . . . The Lord is in debt to no one, so neither will his children be. He alone can pay the price for the salvation of Israel and the establishment of Zion. His wrath is turned away, and he has not cast off the bride or sold her children into slavery.[17]

So, how does this apply to us right here, right now? When someone loses faith, he or she might say, "I just can't feel God in my life. I don't know if I ever did feel God in my life." Sometimes, that person feels like he or she has been deserted by God at a time when He was most needed. Sometimes, this is because of severe trials he or she has had to endure. For whatever reason, this person feels distanced from God. But God is saying, "I didn't walk away from this relationship. I've always been ready to accept you. It was you who turned your back on me."

Then, in other verses, He says, "But [my] hand is stretched out still" (2 Nephi 20:4). In other words, He is saying, "I don't care how far you've strayed from me, how many sins you've committed; I will never forsake you. I will never leave you on your own. But you need to make some effort. You need to turn toward me instead of away from me. Then you will feel my love, and you will know that I never abandoned you. I never left you alone." We need to imagine His hand stretched out to us, and then we will be able to receive the promptings He wants to send us,

---

17. Jeffrey R. Holland, Donald W. Perry, and John W. Welch, "'More Fully Persuaded': Isaiah's Witness of Christ's Ministry," *Isaiah in the Book of Mormon* (Provo: Neal A. Maxwell Institute for Religious Scholarship, 1998), p.11.

whether those promptings come directly from the Holy Ghost or from our own thoughts and feelings.

An acquaintance recounted how his son suffered from a rare, serious, and debilitating disease. The longer his son's trial went on, the less faith my friend had in God until he said:

> I came to a point in my life where I cursed God for allowing my son to suffer so much. That was more than ten years ago, and now things have changed; I realized there was nowhere else to turn. I had nowhere to go for the help I needed. So, I finally woke up and returned to God.

God never departed from him; he departed from God, but he came back, and the Lord was waiting for him with outstretched arms to embrace him.

Later in the seventh chapter of 2nd Nephi, it's as if a faithful child of Israel is responding to the Lord and accepting the Lord's invitation to come unto him, not to turn away from the Lord, not to be ashamed of his belief in the Lord. In verse seven comes another metaphor that is worth understanding—the faithful servant is responding, "For the Lord God will help me, therefore shall I not be confounded. Therefore have I set my face like a flint, and I know that I shall not be ashamed."

What does it mean to "set my face like a flint?" Flint is a very hard rock, harder than steel. That's why when we strike flint against steel, the flint shaves off tiny pieces of iron that catch fire. In this case, the faithful follower of Christ says, "I'm firm. I'm steadfast. I have committed to keep Thy commandments, and I will keep them." It's like my friend when he returned to God and stopped cursing Him.

This is a different image than the hard heart and the stiff neck. Those images connote disobedience. But *a face like flint* means exactly the opposite—someone who turns toward the Lord and does not want to turn away, someone without shame for their beliefs or for their sins. Someone who is all in. My own image of this verse is that when we face God with full commitment, we bask in His light—a light that comes from the unbreakable bond we have with Him, a light that emanates from the love we feel for Him and the love He feels for us. Because we're turning toward Him with a face of flint, the sparks of His light keep lifting us closer to Him and to those we love on earth. A face of flint—a firm commitment—brings breathtaking, beautiful light into our lives.

That light brings us closer to God; our face being like flint can reflect that light to others.

In the final verse of 2 Nephi 7, the Lord warns us against trying to kindle our own light: "Behold all ye that kindle fire, that compass yourselves about with sparks, walk in the light of your fire and in the sparks which ye have kindled. This shall ye have of mine hand—ye shall lie down in sorrow."

My image is of the forlorn soul out in the middle of nowhere, kneeling down and striking his flint and steel against each other to create his own light—like my friend when he turned away from God. He had nowhere else to go. It's like striking flint against steel is his method of dealing with his internal conflicts that keep grinding against each other and causing all kinds of mental anguish.

Here is another image. This one is of the person who turns away from God and indulges in every worldly pleasure imaginable. These people think they see a lot of light because as they stimulate the pleasure center in their brain, and as the stimulation increases, they become hooked on it, and the more hooked they become, the more they want it. When they run out of their own flint or steel, they'll do anything to get more because it brings them momentary release from any problem they face.

When we try to generate our own light by striking our own little piece of flint against our rusting piece of iron, the sparks fly, but they don't create a lasting flame. In time, they burn out, and so do we. We get exhausted trying to create our own light—so much effort for so little light. Rather than hearing the Savior, we hear the noise and confusion of the world. We may use our imagination, but not in compassionate ways.

The Lord's light is different. All we need to do is commit ourselves to turning toward Him, and He will light our way. The firmer we become in our faith, the more our face becomes like flint—always turned toward the Savior. He is not only the one who gives us everlasting light; He is the one who gives us everlasting life. Establishing the Gospel in the early days of the Church, the Lord says in Doctrine and Covenants 10: 66, 70:

> Yea, if they will come, they may, and partake of the waters of life freely. . . . And now, remember the words of him who is the life and light of the world, your Redeemer, your Lord and your God.

So I want to set my face as flint. That takes imagination and compassion. I want to commit to following the Lord every day. I want to turn toward Him so He can spark His light and so I can see it, be lifted by it, and try to lift others by it. I want to hear Him. I want to be filled with His love and help others to be filled as well.

Lolly: We often return from the temple feeling so blessed. It is difficult to describe and explain all that happened to cause those feelings to well up inside. Every week, we experience numerous unexpected encounters with people—performing temple ordinances at the veil, in the initiatory, or in a sealing room. We often feel Heaven close. Sometimes, we encounter an old acquaintance we haven't seen in decades who reminds us of God's goodness. With a name like ours, we are often asked if we are related to someone, and a choice sacred memory is shared. As we've reflected on these chance meetings, we've come to understand they are not by chance but meant to be either for us or the person we met. Elder Jay E. Jensen calls these experiences "divine rendezvous" because of the light emanating from the encounter that always strengthens and lifts. The fact that He gives us these choice experiences in the House of the Lord reminds us of the goodness and love of God.

These divine rendezvous give us exactly the boost we need. The faithful followers of Jesus Christ could have been like the faithful servant in Isaiah 50, who said, "I set my face like a flint." I'm totally committed. Lord, you can count on me. I won't turn you down. I won't turn away. That is my prayer—that I can hear Him and follow Him and help others do the same.

CHAPTER 5
WALK IN THE SPIRIT

WHEN PRESIDENT NELSON PLEADS WITH US TO "HEAR HIM," WE MIGHT think of the revelation we seek as a message from God—words or thoughts coming from the Holy Ghost. But personal revelation does not always come in thoughts; it also comes in feelings. When we feel God's love, we are experiencing personal revelation. We are experiencing a divine message, but not in the form of words or thoughts. When the Lord helps us know that He loves us, we are changed in a most profound way. We come to know Him as He knows us. His embrace surrounds us, and we know that we are more than mere mortals.

In the fifth chapter of Galatians, we learn what it means to walk in the Spirit. Sometimes, we may ask ourselves if we have the Spirit of God with us. Am I listening to the Spirit? Am I following it? Paul teaches the Galatians that it's quite easy to discern if we have the Spirit of the Lord with us because if we do, we will experience the fruit of the Spirit. And what is the fruit? Before answering that, let's review the passages just before the verses where Paul talks about the sins of the flesh; he says they're "manifest"—which means they are quite obviously evil. In verses 19–21, he names some of them:

> Now the works of the flesh are manifest, which are these; Adultery, fornication, uncleanness, lasciviousness, idolatry, witchcraft, hatred, variance, emulations, wrath, strife, seditions, heresies, envyings, murders, drunkenness, revellings, and such like.

Paul's list reminds me of the verse in Mosiah 4:29 where King Benjamin warns his listeners against the works of the flesh, and he summarizes it by saying:

> And finally, I cannot tell you all the things whereby ye may commit sin; for there are divers ways and means, even so many that I cannot number them.

So, after naming these sins, Paul says if we engage in this behavior, we will not inherit the Kingdom of God. If we want to inherit the Kingdom of God, we need to walk in the Spirit. We need to live in the Spirit. And how do we know if the Spirit is with us? How do we know if we're following God? It's quite simple: we experience the fruit of the Spirit. Here are Paul's exact words: "But the fruit of the Spirit is love, joy, peace, longsuffering, gentleness, goodness, faith, meekness, temperance: against such there is no law" (Galatians 5:22–23).

You'll notice that he lists many manifest works of the flesh. The word *works* is plural. And King Benjamin said that the works of the flesh are so numerous that we cannot even name them all. This is important. These scriptures teach us that we can go astray in mortality in so many ways that we cannot even imagine all of them. Technology has led to various evil acts that did not even exist before it invaded every part of our lives. That's why King Benjamin couldn't name all the ways, because he knew that changes in culture and society would lead to more and more ways to go against God.

Now let's look again at what Paul said: "But the fruit of the Spirit is love." He didn't say the fruits of the Spirit are many—so many we cannot name them all. He said "fruit" in the singular. The characteristics that follow the word *love* define the results of love. The pure love of Christ comes from God, and we experience it when we become one with the Savior. Paul is saying there is only one fruit of the Spirit, and that is love. Now, what do I mean by love? I mean joy, peace, longsuffering, gentleness, goodness, faith, meekness, temperance.

We don't usually think of all these things as synonyms for love, but that is what Paul teaches. What do we want more than anything else in mortality? We want to be filled with His love.

Earlier in the First Epistle to the Corinthians, chapter 13, Paul taught that love suffers long and is kind, envieth not, is not puffed up, etc. His list corresponds quite well with the list in Galatians.

The more we hear Him, the more we will feel God's love for us, and the more we feel His love, the more we will want to share that love with others. When we do things out of love, we feel joy and bring joy to others. We feel peace and bring peace to others. We are patient in suffering, and we bring patience to others. We are gentle and never harsh or attacking. Our acts are acts of goodness. And we are humble and meek. This list is such a powerful way to think about divine love.

Love is not a side note in the gospel. Love is not one among many attributes of the Savior. It is the overarching one. It is the one that includes all the other attributes. That's why love is the central message of the first two commandments. All the laws hang on this one divine attribute. Love may be the most important message of all the Godly messages we need.

Love can be our only motive, and when love is our only motive, we don't need to worry about much else. Because we love someone else, we can't take offense at him or her. Because we love others, we can't hurt them. Because we love God, we can't offend Him. Love takes care of everything.

I was thinking about an act of love that was particularly impressive to me. While I was teaching at BYU, a fellow faculty member exhibited early-onset dementia. It came on slowly, so it was hard to detect at first. However, students began to express concern to the department chair about the situation—not in a harsh, complaining way, but with genuine concern that the faculty member was having difficulty teaching the course. "He forgets that he scheduled a quiz, and sometimes he thinks that he handed our assignment back, but he hasn't. We're worried he might have some memory problem."

The department chair had noticed some unusual behavior as well. The intellectually gifted faculty member sometimes seemed to misunderstand or misinterpret things. We all wondered if something was wrong but did not know what it was.

The faculty member was eventually diagnosed with early-onset dementia, and the department chair did something few in his position would have done. He offered to team teach with the faculty member. In other words, he helped him teach every class and helped him with grading—every aspect of the class. The department chair had his classes to teach, but he did this to help the faculty member finish the year so he could leave the university with a more reasonable retirement. Watching this happen, I did not think much of it. I knew the department chair was generous, so it seemed natural. But it was exceptional. It was an act of compassionate imagination. Many would not have imagined doing what he did, and what he did was evidence of his openness to divine inspiration. He was responding to President Nelson's injunction to hear Him. His act of love led to those other attributes in the list that Paul enumerated.

Love is simply the most powerful force in the universe. The adversary has corrupted it in many ways, but he can't undo its ultimate power. Love is the reason Christ atoned for our sins. Love is the essence of His mercy and forgiveness. Love was the reason He created this earth for us, so we could one day live with Him again. His love is infinite and intimate. If we open ourselves to Him, He will fill us with His love. And then we will know we are walking in the Spirit.

CHAPTER 6

EXPERIENCE THE POWER OF STP

One can hear Him in many ways. Because we hear with our ears, we might think that revelation usually comes in words, but it comes perhaps more often as an impression, an image, or a feeling. The question is: How can we sense more impressions, view more images, and experience more feelings from the Lord?

Not long ago, Lolly and I attended general conference, and while we were waiting for the meeting to begin, we began chatting with a young couple seated behind us. Two months after we had met this couple, the sealing coordinator told me that a young man asked to participate in one of my sealing sessions. I did not recognize the name, so I was interested to see how I was acquainted with him.

The time came for the session—there he and his wife were. They had been married for only two weeks and were back in the temple doing sealings for deceased ancestors. I've invited many to join me in the temple, but only a select few respond. This couple came.

Do I worry that this couple will fall into inactivity? No. Do I worry that they're not attending their church meetings on Sunday? No. Do I worry if they're reading their scriptures regularly? No. We got acquainted two months before the sealing session and talked with each other for about 15 minutes. But their commitment to the Lord came through quickly, so I should not have been surprised that they came to my sealing session just as they said they would. This couple, I believe, knows what it means to hear Him!

Lolly: While visiting our family in California, I noticed a bright red and blue sticker that read *STP* on my son-in-law's iPad. I remember this acronym being at my dad's service stations in my youth. It was a gasoline additive that stood for "scientifically treated petroleum." I was curious as to why my son-in-law had this sticker from the past, and he told me this story:

> I don't know if it was general conference, but I just thought that I needed to improve my scripture study, temple, and prayer. I started thinking if there was something I could use to remember that, so I started putting the letters together in my head. When I put *STP*, I remembered the sticker, so I went on Amazon and ordered a few.

After hearing his explanation, we ordered stickers for everybody at our family reunion that year to remind us of our theme. One of our sons and granddaughter even wrote and illustrated a children's book about the boost we get from reading scriptures, worshipping in the temple, and praying. This reminds me of President Nelson's spiritual momentum talk. We all need a little added power every day; scriptures, temple, and prayer will bring that added power.

We will gain added power if we hear the Lord, whether in thoughts, impressions, or feelings. We can sense that added power as we hear Him while we study words in sacred text. We can hear Him as we linger a little longer in the temple's celestial room. We can hear Him as we pray with all the energy of our heart.

While talking with an acquaintance recently who was worried he wasn't feeling the Spirit as much as he would like, I asked him if he was praying. He told me he was not praying as often as he used to. I did not ask him about his temple attendance or scripture reading, but I think he might have wanted or needed to improve those as well. During our conversation, I thought that temporal concerns were taking more time and mental energy than they should. He was not paying enough attention to his spiritual needs.

We all need reminding. We all need to nurture habits that will lead us closer to God: Scriptures, Temple, Prayer. The couple who came to the sealing session are getting a good start to their marriage. They're committed to each other, and they're also committed to the Lord. So, if you feel prompted to improve your scripture reading, your temple worship, or your prayer, I encourage you to think of those three letters—STP—and do it!

CHAPTER 7
PRAY WITHOUT CEASING

I HAVE A FRIEND, ROBERT TODD, AND WE WERE ONCE TALKING ABOUT how he had joined the Church. People often wonder: How does conversion happen? How does someone decide to change their life and be baptized? Well, I found his response particularly compelling. He said, "I remember a sunny day when I was looking out the window of our home. I was in my late teens at the time. And as I gazed out that window, I began to feel that God was aware of me, that I mattered to God. I don't know how else to describe it. But it was a good feeling, a feeling I did not want to end." I responded, "You were feeling the Savior's love." He nodded yes. That experience eventually led him to find the Church and become a member.

My brother Von was less active for 33 years. He not only stopped coming to church, but also lost his belief in God. My brother read my book, *Filled with His Love*, and he called me one day and asked, "So let me see if I get this right—you are saying that if we want our relationships to improve, we need to get closer to God first." I said, "Yes, that's the main point of the book." He said, "Well, I've got a problem; I have no relationship with God."

Gradually, he got closer to God. I accompanied him to the first sacrament meeting he had attended in 33 years, and not long after that, he called me one night. To my surprise, he exclaimed, "I said my first prayer." He had not prayed for such a long time; I was stunned. I asked, "And how did it go?" He said, "I think God was shocked." We both smiled. A few days later we talked again, and he said, "You know, this may sound a little weird, but I kind of want to pray all the time." His discovery made me think of the Bible and Book of Mormon scriptures that encourage us to pray always or without ceasing.

Von's return to the Church had something in common with my friend Robert Todd's initial conversion: each was drawn to God because they felt His love. I like how Von put it: "When you live to love, you love to live!" He began to feel God's love for him and began to feel love for God, so he felt more happiness and gratitude and wanted to pray to Him all the time.

I've thought a lot about what it means to pray without ceasing. Prayer is so essential if we want to hear Him. And if we want the Lord's promptings often, praying without ceasing may be the ultimate key. But what does it mean to "pray without ceasing"? Obviously, we cannot be on our knees 24/7. So we know it does not mean formal prayers with a typical beginning and traditional ending with "amen."

In 3 Nephi 18:15, the Savior teaches his disciples on this continent to pray always: "Verily, verily, I say unto you, ye must watch and pray always, lest ye be tempted by the devil, and ye be led away captive by him."

I believe that the placement of this verse is not by accident. Jesus had just given the sacrament to those close to him and directed his disciples to give the sacrament to every member of the Church. The last phrase in the sacrament prayer is "that they may always have his spirit to be with them." And then he urges them to pray always so that they can resist the buffeting of the adversary.

In 1 Thessalonians 5:16–18, we read: "Rejoice evermore. Pray without ceasing. In every thing give thanks: for this is the will of God in Christ Jesus concerning you." In Mosiah 26:39, a similar admonition is given: "Pray without ceasing, and . . . give thanks in all things." Sometimes we think of prayer as calling upon God for help. These are prayers of asking. But we can also offer prayers of thanks, even with no asking at all—just giving thanks for the blessings we have received and are receiving.

These verses help us see how someone can pray all the time, as my brother expressed to me. Praying without ceasing or praying always is an attitude of the heart. I think that when my friend was looking out his window and feeling God's love, he was engaged in prayer. He didn't know it, but he was. Prayer is two-way communication. He didn't ask for anything directly, but felt God's response to a yearning in his heart.

No words were spoken by him or by God. He had a receptive heart, and God reveals himself to one who is ready and receptive.

Receiving personal revelation, as President Nelson has counseled us to do[18], is in many ways a form of prayer. A new insight, thought, impression, or feeling may come to us unbidden, just as that feeling came to my friend. All we need to do is set our faces as flint and open our hearts and minds, and God will fill us with light.

Praying without ceasing means that we need to have an open heart and open mind all the time. That's a big ask. Sometimes we feel out of sorts, tired, or upset—at these points, we need to ask for help to overcome these feelings. But most of the time, all we need to do is look around us. I'm reminded of the children's song by Newell Dayley, "I Feel My Savior's Love":

> I feel my Savior's love
> In all the world around me.
> His Spirit warms my soul
> Through ev'rything I see.
> He knows I will follow him,
> Give all my life to him.
> I feel my Savior's love,
> The love he freely gives me.

The lyrics of this song describe what my friend felt when looking out his window as a teenager. They also describe what my brother felt when he told me he just wanted to pray all the time. Our love for God and His love for us are the keys to praying always. Our hearts can always be drawn heavenward when we feel God's love for us and express our love to him. And we can express our love for him in many ways. We can serve others. We can give thanks. We can care for the world that he created for us. So many ways—and all those ways cause us to "rejoice evermore" (1 Thessalonians 5:17).

My personal goal is to let my heart rejoice. I want to give more thanks, be more grateful, and call upon the Lord when help is needed. If that thought is always with me—if that feeling is in my soul all day, every day—I truly believe that I will be heeding the admonition to pray always.

---

18. Russell M. Nelson, *Revelation for the Church, Revelation for Our Lives*, General Conference, The Church of Jesus Christ of Latter-day Saints, Apr. 2018, Gospel Library App.

CHAPTER 8

WRITE THE LORD'S NAME ON YOUR HEART

ONE WAY WE CAN HEAR HIM IS TO COMMIT THE LORD'S WORDS TO memory, and then we can review them at any time. I once talked with Joseph Fielding McConkie, son of Elder Bruce R. McConkie. He told me about a conversation with a student who asked, "What tips do you have for me so that I can know the gospel as well as your dad did?" Joseph McConkie tried to help the student understand that there was no shortcut or set of tips to develop the kind of gospel understanding Elder McConkie had accomplished over a lifetime. He explained to the student that even at an early age, Elder McConkie had studied the scriptures in such depth that when attending university, he would daily create ten-minute talks on different doctrines. He found that it took at least ten minutes to walk between classes, so once he had developed a talk in his mind, he would practice it on his way to the next class.

Joseph McConkie was trying to help the student understand that this was one way his father had written the word of God on his heart. The scriptures were not in a book on the shelf; they were deep down inside Elder McConkie.

When raising our children, my wife and I tried to help them get the scriptures inside their hearts. We would post a verse on the refrigerator and work at meal and prayer times during the week to memorize it. The following is a conversation my wife and I had on how we tried to write the word of God on our hearts.

Russ: We often use the phrase "learn by heart," which means "commit to memory." Interestingly, we don't say "learn by mind" or "learn by brain." Since the heart is the seat of emotion and the center of the spirit, committing sacred text to memory differs from memorizing the periodic table in chemistry or the times tables in math. God's word can change us, lift us, and strengthen us—to help us draw close to Him. Scripture memorization definitely can't be forced. Those who memorize need to do it because they want to do it. But it has been our experience that once a child commits a verse to memory, that child wants to memorize more. They recognize even at an early age that these words have power—sacred, holy power—and they want to be able to say them without opening a book of scripture.

Lolly: My mother set the example—the way she woke me every morning for early morning seminary with these words from Doctrine and Covenants section 88: "See that ye love one another; cease to be covetous; learn to impart one to another as the gospel requires" (verse 123). Then, with a markedly louder voice, she would say, "Cease to be idle; cease to be unclean . . . cease to sleep longer than is needful" (verse 124). She would pause at that point until I was awake and then say the reminder of the passage with all the power of a great prophet, such as King Benjamin standing on his tower:

> Retire to thy bed early, that ye may not be weary; arise early, that your bodies and your minds may be invigorated. And above all things, clothe yourselves with the bond of charity, as with a mantle, which is the bond of perfectness and peace. Pray always, that ye may not faint, until I come. Behold, and lo, I will come quickly, and receive you unto myself (D&C 88:124–126).

Those verses have stayed with me all my life. I remember my mother reciting this scripture for four years every morning I attended seminary. It's no wonder I memorized it! These verses were written on my heart, and I wanted to help our children get the scriptures inside them—written on their hearts.

One of the first verses we memorized as a family were King Benjamin's words: "And ye will not suffer your children that they go hungry, or naked; neither will ye suffer that they transgress the laws of God, and fight and quarrel one with another, and serve the devil" (Mosiah 4:14). So whenever our kids started fighting with each other, we would gently ask them to recite this scripture. It worked.

Russ: And in recent years, at family reunions, we all memorize in our families a chosen verse before the reunion and then recite it together during the reunion at our nightly devotionals. For example, "Look unto me in every thought; doubt not, fear not" (Doctrine & Covenants 6:36). "Be of good cheer; it is I; be not afraid" (Matthew 14:27). "Look forward with an eye of faith" (Alma 5:15). "Let virtue garnish thy thoughts unceasingly" (Doctrine & Covenants 121:45). And "Can ye look up to God at that day with a pure heart and clean hands? . . . Can you look up, having the image of God engraven upon your countenances?" (Alma 5:19).

Lolly: One of our daughters had her children rehearse their monthly family scripture as she drove them to school each morning. One month, I remember they memorized the charity scripture in Moroni 7. All occupants of the carpool, including the neighbor kids, memorized scripture together. We would get a video call periodically on their way to school, reciting their memorized scripture.

Russ: I've been amazed how even young children can commit scripture to memory. Some even as young as four did a great job, and a two-year-old mumbling along with an occasional intelligible word or two was a delight to see.

Lolly: When they go on missions, they use one of the scriptures they learned when they were young to be the basis of an extemporaneous talk.

Russ: Like Elder McConkie practicing his talks on the way to his next class at the university.

Lolly: Exactly. When God's words are written on your heart, you can draw on them whenever you need them to lift others.

Russ: I love the words in Proverbs 3:3: "Let not mercy and truth forsake thee: bind them about thy neck; write them upon the table of thine heart."

Lolly: That verse reminds me of the song we sang in our own family growing up and now at our family reunions with grandchildren: "Write Thy Blessed Name, O Lord, Upon My Heart." I tell my family in all seriousness that I want them to sing this hymn at my funeral. The words were written by a Catholic scholar, Thomas à Kempis, in the Middle

Ages. But though it was written so long ago, these words speak to me now:

> Write Your blessed name,
> O Lord, upon my heart,
> There to remain so indelibly engraved,
> That no prosperity, That no adversity
> Shall ever move me from Your love.[19]

Russ: Those final words: "that no prosperity, no adversity shall ever move me from Your love," describe the kind of oneness we want to have with the Lord because both prosperity and adversity can move us away from God. This is a fervent prayer, much like Mormon asked in Moroni 7:48: "Pray unto the Father with all the energy of heart, that ye may be filled with this love." This entire song is a prayer of divine oneness, a plea to the Father that His name written on our hearts takes precedence over everything else in our lives—our problems, successes, worries, and delights. Everything.

Lolly: Yes, everything! I'm convinced that when God's words are written on our hearts, we will have the strength to withstand whatever comes to us. This is one way we can hear Him every day. When His words are inside us, our minds are more open to inspiration from heaven. When the words of the world take over, we lose touch with heaven and close our minds. But when we reflect on the truths in the scriptures, we feel His love and open ourselves to the personal revelation God is so eager to pour out upon us. This is what compassionate imagination is all about—being able to receive the inspiration we need to live as the Lord wants us to live.

---

19. Dale Grotenhuis and Thomas à Kempis, "Write Your Blessed Name," (Dayton, Ohio: The Sacred Music Press, 1991).

CHAPTER 9

DON'T LIVE BY BREAD ALONE

COMPASSIONATE IMAGINATION SHIFTS OUR THINKING AWAY FROM THE momentary, material world and lifts our gaze to eternity. That means trading in our natural-man-and-woman tendency that causes us to fixate on our possessions to a higher and holier nature as offspring of God. We don't want to be possessed by our possessions; we want to be possessed by God. That is when we strengthen our ability to hear Him.

As I was studying the fourth chapters of Matthew and Luke, I reflected on my childhood. For the first nine years of my life, I lived across the fence from the Gordon B. Hinckley home. I might have spent more time in their home during my early years than in my own. Sister Hinckley was like a second mother to me. She always talked to me the same way she spoke to her son Clark, my best friend as a youth.

One day while in their home, Clark and I went into their study, a room that was constructed on what had once been a concrete patio. (President Hinckley was the king of home improvements—always remodeling, moving the kitchen, making a new bedroom in their garage, and gluing wallpaper to a newly built room.) So here we were in their study. Lots of built-in shelves filled with books that surrounded the room. More books than I had ever encountered inside anyone's home.

I began scanning the shelves to see if there was a title that jumped out at me. One of the books was *Not by Bread Alone* by Bryant S. Hinckley. I couldn't believe it! A book written by someone I knew personally. Bryant S. Hinckley was Gordon B. Hinckley's father and lived a few minutes' walk behind their home. My father had been Bryant S. Hinckley's home teaching companion. And my mother grew up very close to his farm. I called him Papa Hinckley because that's what Clark called him. Whenever we saw him, he would give me a dime and encourage me to put it in my mission fund. He was a kindly old gentleman with hair as white as President McKay's.

So there I was, looking at his book on the shelf. I opened the cover and began reading. After a few minutes, I placed it back on the shelf where I had found it and felt a little better, a little lighter, a little more capable. I don't know why. The book just lifted me. And I was probably only about twelve years old.

Recently, while reading in the Book of Luke, I saw the phrase that became the title of Bryant S. Hinckley's book: "And the devil said unto him, If thou be the Son of God, command this stone that it be made bread. And Jesus answered him, saying, It is written, that man shall not live by bread alone, but by every word of God" (Luke 4:3–4).

Then I wondered—is that book still available after all these years? It was first published in 1955 and then reprinted again later. So I went to my Deseret Book library and tracked it down. Yes, it's still available, even on Amazon—68 years after it was released. I got the e-book version and began to read. This is what I found in the introduction:

> Thou shalt not live by bread alone (Luke 4:4). Man himself is the crowning wonder of creation. A study of his nature—the noblest study the world affords (Gladstone).
>
> "Thou shalt not live by bread alone," is a divine command. Man cannot live without bread, but he has a higher hunger, a longing for better things, which sets him apart as the crowning wonder of creation. This places upon him the obligation of growing as long as he lives. To do this, he needs the stimulation that comes from great ideals, from a steadfast faith, and the inspiration that comes from contact with high-powered souls. Hard work and high thinking are the price of the most worth-while accomplishments. The purpose of this book is to awaken and stimulate the forces that lead to happy and victorious living.[20]

---

20. Bryant S. Hinckley, *Not by Bread Alone* (Salt Lake City: Bookcraft, 1955), p.iii.

The account in the fourth chapters of Matthew and Luke is a powerful explanation of what it means to resist the world—the constant urge to satisfy our physical needs—and look to God for our sustenance—our spiritual food.

There is much irony in these chapters. Jesus has a desire to prepare for His earthly ministry, so He goes into the wilderness in fasting and prayer. But then Satan appears and tempts Him after He has fasted so long. His strength must have been nearly depleted, and Satan asks Jesus to turn the stone into bread, so He can eat. But Jesus was stronger than Satan. His body may have been frail, but His spirit was strong. And that's when He said, "Man shall not live by bread alone" (Matthew 4:4). Jesus was spiritually close to His Father in Heaven, and that closeness gave Him the strength to command Satan to depart.

God's words lift and strengthen us. Bread satisfies our hunger for an hour or two, but God's words can lift us daily if we let them.

Now, back to the study in the Hinckley home. When President Hinckley's father published his book, President Hinckley was 45 years old. He had not yet been called as a general authority and would not be sustained as President of the Church for another 40 years. But he had grown up in a home where his parents knew the difference between the need to satisfy physical desires and the need to fill ourselves with the love of God.

We often receive ads in the mail for a great deal on a new credit card. One caught my eye, entitled "Bread Cash-Back." I thought about why they used the word *bread*. Well, it's pretty simple: "bread" is slang for "money"—especially in British slang, as the word *dough* refers to money. So the card could have been called "Money Cash-Back Card."

I think that's what is meant in the scriptures. To say we don't live by bread alone is to say that money is not enough. It doesn't matter how much money you have; it will never be enough. But God's word, God's love, is eternal. It will never disappear. All we need to do is seek it, accept it, treasure it, and live it.

Now, I want to return to Bryant S. Hinckley's inclusion of a quote by William Gladstone, a former prime minister of England: "Man himself is the crowning wonder of creation. A study of his nature—the noblest study the world affords."[21]

---

21. Hinckley, *Not by Bread Alone*, p.iii.

As God's children, we are the crowning wonder of creation. Not money. Not any material good. And a study of the nature of God's children is the noblest study the world affords. That's why we need to be constantly looking at how we think, how we feel, how we relate to each other, and how we attach ourselves to God. The more we can understand our divine nature, the closer we will draw to our Maker and the closer we will draw to each other—oneness with God and unity with all others. That is where compassionate imagination leads us. Our nature is not simply mortal. We are eternal beings living in mortality. We must imagine our eternal destiny and act with compassion to experience it.

The Heart Approach—E: Envision Oneness and Christlike Unity

Some might say that, as a nation, we have never been as divided as we are now. The January 6 Capitol riot is emblematic of the divisiveness that has been brewing for decades. We are not only a long way from being of one heart; we can hardly talk to one another without argument and dissension. Oneness? Zion? Unity? These are difficult to imagine. But we must imagine them, or we will remain divided forever. Division leads to dissolution and destruction. Oneness leads to understanding and peace. We need compassionate imagination if we want to become one with God and be unified with others. We first must conceive the image, then we need to create the compassion. The wonder of the word *compassion* is that it is not simply an inert feeling that leaves us sitting around doing nothing. Compassion leads to action—a type of action that is born of love.

Lehi had a vision of the Tree of Life, and one of the most powerful scenes in the dream—a dream in which all scenes are powerful—is the image of Lehi immediately after he tastes the fruit of the Tree of Life. What is his first thought once he knows how desirable the fruit is? He wants his family to partake. So he begins looking for them afar off. He sees Sam, Nephi, and his wife. And he notices that they seem unsure of where to go:

> At the head thereof I beheld your mother Sariah, and Sam, and Nephi; and they stood as if they knew not whither they should go. And it came to pass that I beckoned unto them; and I also did say unto them with a loud voice that they should come unto me, and

partake of the fruit, which was desirable above all other fruit. And it came to pass that they did come unto me and partake of the fruit also (1 Nephi 8:14–16).

At the beginning of the vision in verse 6, Lehi sees the Savior: "And it came to pass that he spake unto me, and bade me follow him." We no longer use the verb *bid* in a sense of asking or inviting. We would not say, "He bade me come to dinner." However, if we examine the former use of the word, we see that it is a special kind of invitation—it meant to "entreat" or "beg" or "pray" the person to come. To entreat means to ask with earnestness.[22] It's not a casual form of invitation. It's heartfelt, just as Ruth said to Naomi, "Entreat me not to leave thee" (Ruth 1:16).

Lehi's vision was given to him in mental imagery. He saw the Tree of Life in his mind, and then reached out to his family in compassion. Truth from God always leads to compassionate action. His wife and two of his children gladly accepted his invitation and came and partook of the Tree—the Love of God. But two of his sons declined. I believe that one of the most powerful messages of Lehi's vision is the importance of oneness. His vision occurred long before the Lamanites separated from the Nephites and began to attack each other. However, the seeds of divisiveness were there long before: in the wilderness, on the ship, in the promised land. Brotherly envy and strife were present all along, and Lehi worried about that perhaps more than anything else. He wanted his family to be unified—to love one another. And he knew that his children first needed to feel oneness with God; only then could they unite as a family.

In this section of the book, I will suggest ways that we can envision oneness with God and Christlike unity with others. If we are ever to establish Zion, this oneness and unity must lead us there. We have very little knowledge of how Enoch and his city achieved it, but we know that they did, which means that oneness with God and Christlike unity with others is possible. If we practice compassionate imagination, we can feel that oneness and experience that unity. I hope that each of the following chapters will help us do that.

---

22. "Bid Definition &Meaning," definition 2b and 2c, Merriam-Webster, https://www.merriam-webster.com/dictionary/bid.

CHAPTER 10
EXAMINE YOUR MOTIVES

COMPASSIONATE IMAGINATION ALWAYS LEADS TO RIGHTEOUS ACTION—not just any type of action, but righteous action. What is righteous action? Any action motivated by the pure love of Christ. There are many ways to read the Sermon on the Mount. In my study, I began thinking of the Lord's underlying message throughout chapters 6 and 7 of Matthew. I see in the meta-message of the Savior's revolutionary sermon that motives matter. In other words, what we do is less important than why we do it. When we act out of love, our actions will lead toward God because God embodies infinite love.

Let's begin with the first verse in Matthew 6: "Take heed that ye do not your alms before men, to be seen of them." So Jesus wants us to do alms—in other words, serve Him—but He wants us to serve Him for the right reason: because we love Him, not because we want others to praise us. Motives matter.

Then later in verse 5 of the same chapter, He teaches us the same principle about how we pray: "And when thou prayest, thou shalt not be as the hypocrites are: for they love to pray standing in the synagogues and in the corners of the streets, that they may be seen of men." Again, Jesus is helping us see that the reason we pray is more important than the prayer itself. We might say many nice words in a prayer, but if we are saying those words to sound pious, righteous, or devoted so that others will think better of us, our prayer is in vain. Motives matter.

Then He teaches us the same thing again about fasting in verse 16: "Moreover when ye fast, be not, as the hypocrites, of a sad countenance:

for they disfigure their faces, that they may appear unto men to fast." Again, going without food has no value unless we dedicate our fast to God—unless we do it out of love for God. Motives matter.

Jesus makes clear the motive that we should have in all aspects of our worship: "The light of the body is the eye: if therefore thine eye be single"—and the Prophet Joseph added "to the glory of God" in the JST version—"thy whole body shall be full of light" (Matthew 6:22). So if our thoughts and hearts are aimed toward God out of love, our worship will fill us with God's light and love.

Later in Matthew 7:22–23, Jesus summarizes His central message: "Many will say to me in that day, Lord, Lord, have we not prophesied in thy name? and in thy name have cast out devils? and in thy name done many wonderful works? And then will I profess unto them, I never knew you [this reads "ye never knew me" in the Joseph Smith Translation]: depart from me, ye that work iniquity."

This is the grand summary principle. Jesus is teaching that people can do many things that appear to be good and wholesome on the outside. They can teach good lessons, give good talks, write uplifting messages—but if they do any of those things for the wrong reason—for outward praise, monetary reward, or any other worldly motive—it counts for naught. They may have preached a good sermon, but did not do it out of love for the Lord. They never really came to know God because their motives were corrupt.

Then comes this most important statement: "Therefore all things whatsoever ye would that men should do to you, do ye even so to them: for this is the law and the prophets" (Matthew 7:12). Here, Jesus is saying that first, we need to do all we do out of love for God since our eye is single to His glory. Then, going back to the first two commandments, we need to do all those things out of real love for our neighbor. Motives matter.

What does all this mean for us? We may need to spend a little more time examining our motives. We can do a good act simply to get it done, or we can do it out of love for God and for others. We focus so much on what we are trying to accomplish that we sometimes fail to look at the motives underlying our actions. The more we look at our motives, the more we will do what we do out of love for God and for others, and the more we do that, the more we will come to know the Lord. Then we won't be among those to whom Jesus said, "Ye never knew me." Motives matter. They matter a lot. This is one of the overriding messages of the Sermon on the Mount, a sermon that changed the world.

Compassionate imagination is one answer to the challenge we have with motives. When we decide to help someone, we use our imagination to decide what to do. In essence, we see ourselves doing the act before we do it. If we decide to visit someone who is convalescing from a serious illness, we imagine what we will do before we do it. Will we take flowers, a book, or nothing at all? When will be the best time? Should we call before we go? There are lots of little decisions to make before we act. And if compassion underlies all our decisions, then we know our motives are pure. When Ruth and Orpah asked Naomi to please let them come along to the land of Judah, the plea was out of love for Naomi—compassion. They wanted to be unified with her. Ruth said, "Thy people shall be my people, and thy God my God" (Ruth 1:16). Oneness with God and Christlike unity with others—this is the result of compassionate imagination.

CHAPTER 11
BECOME LIKE GOD

JESUS PRAYED THAT WE WOULD ALL BECOME ONE WITH GOD AS HE AND the Father are one. Oneness with God means becoming like Him. While some religious traditions view God as mystical and unknowable, Latter-day Saints know that God the Father, His Son, and the Holy Ghost are three separate beings we can know and love. In Acts 17:22–23, we read that when Paul was preaching to the Athenians from Mars Hill, he found an inscription: "TO THE UNKNOWN GOD." His goal was to help the Athenians discard their previous notions of God, to help them understand that God is knowable. He was trying to teach them the true nature of God. This was also a central mission of the Prophet Joseph Smith in this dispensation—to help all who would embrace the Restored Gospel of Jesus Christ understand God's true nature.

Here's the essential point: when we come to understand the true nature of God, we also come to understand our true nature because we are His offspring. As Paul taught in Acts 17:27–29,

> That they should seek the Lord, if haply they might feel after him, and find him, though he be not far from every one of us: For in him we live, and move, and have our being; as certain also of your own poets have said, For we are also his offspring. Forasmuch then as we are the offspring of God, we ought not to think that the Godhead is like unto gold, or silver, or stone, graven by art and man's device.

He taught the Athenians that God is not some mysterious being, inaccessible to humans. Rather, he is not far off from all of us. He is our

Father. His purpose is to help his children. The graven images that the Athenians worshipped at that time were not God, and they needed to shift their focus to God, who is their literal Father.

I love verse 28: "For in [God] we live, and move, and have our being." He gives us breath just as He breathed life into Adam. And what does it mean to breathe life into another? It means to inspire. A meaning of the word *inspire* is "to breathe in," as shown in the Oxford English Dictionary. We now think of it as a form of revelation, and that it is. We are inhaling the breath that God breathes into us. So today, when you breathe in some fresh air, think of how the Lord provided that air for you and how He is breathing life into you and, through that, will help you do what you were meant to do today.

We are the offspring of God. And that means we can become like Him because He is our Father. As Mormon taught in Moroni 7:47–48, when we are filled with His love and learn how to love as He loves, we can become like Him. And that is the whole purpose of mortality.

Some in historical Christianity have seen this doctrine as blasphemous. They think that it brings God down to our level. However, if we interpret it correctly, we begin to see that we can become like God, rather than God becoming like us. We see our life as more exalting with more capacity to develop the holiness that God possesses.

Lorenzo Snow taught this doctrine—that we could become like God—throughout his life. Here's an excerpt from chapter 5 of *Teachings of Presidents of the Church: Lorenzo Snow*:

> In the spring of 1840, Lorenzo Snow was in Nauvoo, Illinois, preparing to leave for a mission in England. He visited the home of his friend Henry G. Sherwood, and he asked Brother Sherwood to explain a passage of scripture . . . "The Spirit of the Lord rested mightily upon me—the eyes of my understanding were opened, and I saw as clear as the sun at noonday, with wonder and astonishment, the pathway of God and man. I formed the following couplet which expresses the revelation, as it was shown me. ...
>
> "As man now is, God once was:
>
> "As God now is, man may be."
>
> Feeling that he had received "a sacred communication" that he should guard carefully, Lorenzo Snow did not teach the doctrine publicly until he knew that the Prophet Joseph Smith had taught

it. Once he knew the doctrine was public knowledge, he testified of it frequently.[23]

If you want to take a deep dive into this doctrine, check out Andrew Skinner's book, *To Become Like God: Witnesses of Our Divine Potential*. Andrew Skinner is a former dean of religious education at BYU. In this book, he recounts how this doctrine has ancient as well as modern origins. Members of other Christian churches who disagree with this doctrine may not realize that the doctrine was in their religions long ago.

Here's an excerpt from Skinner's book. Skinner calls the doctrine "deification"—becoming like God. And he quotes ancient theologians who taught the doctrine very clearly:

> For example, Clement of Alexandria (circa 150–215) became head of an institution devoted to instruction in Christian doctrine. For Clement, Jesus Christ was the source of all reason and understanding. But more important, "The Word of God became man, that thou mayest learn from man how man may become God." Furthermore, "His is beauty, the true beauty, for it is God; and that man becomes God, since God so wills. Heraclitus, then, rightly said, 'men are gods, and gods are men.' Clement said, "He who listens to the Lord, and follows the prophecy [teachings] given by Him, will be formed perfectly in the likeness of the teacher—made a god going about in flesh."[24]

Then Skinner draws upon the preaching of President Lorenzo Snow:

> We were born in the image of God our Father; He begot us like unto himself. There is the nature of deity in the composition of our spiritual organization; in our spiritual birth our Father transmitted to us the capabilities, powers and faculties which he himself possessed, as much so as the child on its mother's bosom possesses, although in an undeveloped state, the faculties, powers and susceptibilities of its parent.[25]

For most of us, it takes a great deal of imagination to see ourselves becoming like God. We need to envision it. We are often more likely

---

23. *Teachings of Presidents of the Church: Lorenzo Snow* (Salt Lake City: The Church of Jesus Christ of Latter-day Saints, 2012), p.83.

24. Andrew C. Skinner, *To Become Like God: Witnesses of Our Divine Potential* (Salt Lake City: Deseret Book Company, 2016), chapters 6 and 9.

25. Ibid.

to see our faults and weaknesses than we are to see our divine potential. But this is doctrinally sound. We can become like God. President Nelson has taught that "perfection is pending,"[26] so we know that we will not become like God in this life. However, we need to be moving in that direction. Here's where I think compassionate imagination comes into play. We need to be compassionate with others, but we also need to have self-compassion. We need to forgive ourselves and imagine that we can change and improve. The more we hear Him and have His image "engraven upon [our] countenances" (Alma 5:19), the more we will envision our divine destiny. Compassionate imagination can help us become like God.

---

26. Russell M. Nelson, *Perfection Pending*, General Conference, The Church of Jesus Christ of Latter-day Saints, Oct. 1995, Gospel Library App.

CHAPTER 12

KNOW THAT YOU ARE ABSOLUTELY ESSENTIAL

FOR MOST, IT IS EASIER TO ENVISION JESUS GROWING FROM "GRACE TO grace" (Doctrine and Covenants 93:13) than to envision ourselves gradually becoming perfected through His Atonement. Our weaknesses are evident, and our strengths are sometimes hard to see. Then, envisioning Christlike unity with others can be even more daunting because we sometimes see others as more essential, more capable than ourselves. The power to envision is indispensable for the development of our compassionate imagination.

Speaking to the saints in Corinth, Paul said:

For as the body is one, and hath many members, and all the members of that one body, being many, are one body: so also is Christ. For by one Spirit are we all baptized into one body, whether we be Jews or Gentiles, whether we be bond or free; and have been all made to drink into one Spirit (1 Corinthians 12:12–13).

His message is clear: we can be united and still be unique individuals with our likes, dislikes, talents, gifts, and capacities. Paul is describing just how different we can be from one another. And the central message is that our differences must not separate us.

The first time I visited China, I stood outside the Beijing Hotel waiting for a driver to pick me up. I had been in the city for only a few days, but I was overcome with the feeling that everyone should experience other cultures. Stereotyping, labeling, and diminishing people is so easy when we have not lived with them and come to understand them. Paul is reminding us in a powerful way that it doesn't matter where we grew up, our skin color, our gender, our income level, or what we prefer to eat. When we enter the waters of baptism, we become one with each other:

> For the body is not one member, but many. If the foot shall say, Because I am not the hand, I am not of the body; is it therefore not of the body? And if the ear shall say, Because I am not the eye, I am not of the body; is it therefore not of the body? (1 Corinthians 12:14–16).

These verses make me think about those who feel left out, discarded, unappreciated, or lonely. They look at others and envy them for some characteristic, talent, or gift they have. But Paul is pleading with the Saints to look for the good in others, and just because someone else has a good singing voice or is a star athlete, that doesn't mean that we need to sing as well as they do or put a basketball in a hoop or cook or write as well as they do. They are needed, but so are we.

A friend once said, "The worst thing about growing older is that you don't feel like your ideas count anymore. No one wants to listen to you because they have others they would rather listen to." We all need to help each other every day feel absolutely essential, just as the eye and the ear are to the body. We need to know that others look to us for help. When Lolly and I were serving as mission leaders, we felt needed—some days, too much so. Missionaries would call with all kinds of problems and questions: physical illness, emotional problems, companion relationships, and on and on. Why couldn't we all feel that needed all the time? You might be saying to yourself—I feel *too* needed sometimes. I wish I felt less needed. If you're saying that, I believe you're in the minority. Too many people feel undervalued.

The other day, I was sitting in a waiting room and struck up a conversation with a man sitting a few seats away from me. I said, "Your wife said she's a school psychologist, and what do you do for a living?"

He shrugged his shoulders and said, "Just construction," as if construction weren't a worthy occupation. I asked, "So, what's your favorite thing to do in construction?"

"The toys," he said.

"Toys?" I asked. It shows how much I know about how people talk about construction work.

"Yeah," he responded. "The big trucks, the front loaders, you know." I said, "You do excavation work."

"Yeah," he said. I then explained how my son, when his family's new home was being built, liked the excavation work more than any construction phase. I went on to tell him how enamored my son was with the guy who ran the big machines that moved all the earth that needed to be moved before they could begin the building process.

On the way home, I began thinking about our own home and how essential it is to our lives. I wanted to go back and talk to that man again and tell him how essential he is—that his job is more important than he thinks. *He's* more important than he thinks. We can't live without a roof over our heads or get a roof over our heads unless someone prepares the ground for the home to be built. He might see himself as the foot rather than the head, but the body can't move without the foot. After all, "if the whole body were an eye, where were the hearing? If the whole were hearing, where were the smelling?" (1 Corinthians 12:17).

Think how boring life would be if we were all identical to one another. It is our differences that make life so rich. So rather than allowing our differences to drive us apart, we need to value each other because of our uniqueness.

> But now hath God set the members every one of them in the body, as it hath pleased him. And if they were all one member, where were the body? But now are they many members, yet but one body (1 Corinthians 12:18–20).

So we all must feel needed—not just needed, but absolutely essential—as if the world could not exist without us. When my grandmother died after a long and fruitful life, my dad walked over to me during the luncheon held after her funeral. He had tears in his eyes, which he didn't have very often. He put his hand on my shoulder as if to receive a little support from me and said, "She's gone. Life will never be the same." He was beginning the mourning process that naturally follows the death of a loved one. And he was right; life never would be the same. She was his only parent. His father passed away when my father was four years old. And now his mother was gone. And he couldn't quite come to grips with it. She had been the mainstay, the anchor, the one everyone in the family leaned on. She was quiet but so strong. And now she was gone. He had always known, as I had, that she was essential and needed, but now that she was gone, he felt it even more strongly, so strongly he could hardly bear it.

So while we are among the living, we need to ensure that those we love know how much we love them, how essential they are to us, and how needed they are. Children need to know this, youth need to know it, young parents need to know it, and the aging need to know it. Paul was teaching the Corinthians that they needed to envision themselves as essential as well as more important than they had previously thought. This envisioning is a critical part of compassionate imagination. We need to engage in it every day. My prayer is that we can envision our own importance as well as convey to others just how essential they are to us and our happiness—absolutely essential. The more we do that, the more oneness we will experience.

CHAPTER 13
CHANGE YOUR DESIRES

IF WE CAN COME TO KNOW THAT WE ARE ABSOLUTELY ESSENTIAL IN God's plan, and if we can envision ourselves becoming like God, then we might agree that we must make a few personal changes. We need to repent. But if we are to improve our behavior, we need to change our desires. Is it possible for us to change our desires? God knows it is, but do we know it?

In Luke chapter 19, we read about the encounter Jesus had with Zacchæus, a wealthy man so eager to meet Jesus that he climbed a sycamore tree to see Jesus as he passed by. Jesus visited Zacchæus in his home, and others murmured and said that Jesus should not go to the home of a sinner, but He could see that Zacchæus was a devoted man whose heart was right. As it says in the Doctrine and Covenants, "For I, the Lord, will judge all men according to their works, according to the desire of their hearts (Doctrine and Covenants 137:9)."

This verse implies that the desires in our hearts precede all human actions. So if our desires are righteous, then our actions will be righteous. It all begins with desire.

One of the greatest paradoxes in mortality is that, as humans, we often do the opposite of what we know is good for us—texting while driving, eating three brownies while trying to lose weight, and becoming angry at someone we love. None of these actions makes sense. Simple logic would dictate that we make a different decision in every case. But simple logic is not the most important determinant of human action. No, there is a stronger determinant of human conduct than logic alone.

What is it? Human desire. We act on our desires most of the time. We do what we want to do, and sometimes that's not what we should do. So the pressing question is: Can we change our desires?

Let's put this question into perspective. It is not just an interesting question to think about; it's one of the most important questions we can consider. If human desires can change, then moral agency is everything. If human desires cannot change, then moral agency means nothing.

To show how pivotal this question is, consider this excerpt from an article that appeared in USA Today. The author is a respected professor of biology. Here's how he begins his essay, "Why You Don't Have Free Will"[27]:

> Perhaps you've chosen to read this essay after scanning other articles on this website. Or, if you're in a hotel, maybe you've decided what to order for breakfast or what clothes you'll wear today.
> You haven't.

This is an important assertion. The author's saying that you didn't actually make the decisions you thought you made. You did not choose the choices you thought you made. He continues:

> You may *feel* like you've made choices, but in reality your decision to read this piece, and whether to have eggs or pancakes, was determined long before you were aware of it—perhaps even before you woke up today. And your "will" had no part in that decision.

We might equate the word *will* here with agency. He is saying that agency does not really exist. He continues to drive his point home:

> So it is with all of our other choices: not one of them results from a free and conscious decision on our part. There is no freedom of choice, no free will. And those New Year's resolutions you made? You had no choice about making them, and you'll have no choice about whether you keep them.

Those are pretty strong words. But these thoughts are not unique to this author. One more excerpt from his article:

---

27. Jerry A. Coyne, "Why You Don't Really Have Free Will," http://www. thinking-differently.com/phil001/wp-content/uploads/2013/03/Readings_ free_will.pdf.

And that's what neurobiology is telling us: Our brains are simply meat computers that, like real computers, are programmed by our genes and experiences to convert an array of inputs into a predetermined output.

So rather than viewing ourselves as eternal beings with a spirit and a body that together compose the soul, some assert that we are simply "meat computers" pre-programmed by our genes and environment.

Think for a moment how appealing this argument is. We have no control whatsoever over our genes. And the way this argument portrays experiences, we have no control over those either. If we have no responsibility for our actions, what does it matter whether we do good or evil? Or is there even a difference between good and evil if decisions don't matter at all?

You might be saying to yourself now, "Of course, there is a difference between good and evil, and of course, we have responsibility for our actions. People change." Something else is at play here, something else very important. It is the foundational doctrine of the plan of salvation. We've grown up with it as members of the Church of Jesus Christ of Latter-day Saints. We learn at an early age that we do make decisions. We know that we are responsible for our actions. Nephi taught us "to act . . . and not to be acted upon" (2 Nephi 2:26).

Moral agency is an essential, fundamental doctrine of the restored gospel of Jesus Christ. It is what the war in heaven was fought over. It gives us the possibility of personal growth—becoming more like the Savior. It underlies everything. There's only one problem: we don't always use our agency to choose the right. There is always a gap between what we know we should do and what we actually do.

That brings us back to desire. Our desires give rise to our choices and our decisions. If we could just change our desires, the gap would diminish. We would do what we know we should do, because we want to do what we should. So can we change our desires? If our desires can change, we can simply tell ourselves to desire the good, and we will always choose the good. However, I don't think it's that simple. If you've ever tried to lose weight, gain weight, or spend less time on social media, you know that it takes more than a one-minute conversation with yourself to change your desires.

Lolly: Several years ago, we attended a training meeting for CES seminary and institute instructors broadcast from Salt Lake. President Dallin H. Oaks was presiding and introduced his concluding remarks with his journey of learning the importance of prayer and scripture study. He told of how he reads several newspapers and other reading materials daily to keep abreast of the world, but described how he would never think of *not* praying before studying his scriptures. When he said that, I thought about how I'd never even considered praying before reading my scriptures. A bit chagrined, on the drive back home, I mentioned to Russ my folly, and he concurred. We both decided right then to always pray from then on before our daily scripture study. We both agreed to help each other remember to do it.

Now in practice, it took a lot of starts and then start-agains. Because we had read scriptures together for so many years without praying, we would sometimes be halfway through our study before one of us would interrupt, "We forgot to pray!" It was more difficult than we had thought. President Oaks's challenge sounded easy, but it wasn't. It took nearly three months of "practice" before it became easier. We helped each other do something we both wanted to do. This mutual goal and continual effort have made sincere prayer automatic. Each morning, as we express gratitude for the scriptures and ask for help understanding them, we find nuggets of joy for us individually and as a couple.

The important message here is that human beings can change. We can decide to do what we know we should do. We can act on our desires, and our desires can become stronger and more focused on the good. During the October 2012 priesthood session, President Monson said clearly: "We need to bear in mind that people can change. They can put behind them bad habits. . . . We must develop the capacity to see men not as they are at present but as they may become when they receive testimonies of the gospel of Christ."[28]

There are only two positions we can take in life. The first says that our brains are like "meat computers." The second says that we are eternal beings with the power to choose good from evil. The first position means that we are not responsible for our actions. The second means that we

---

28. Thomas S. Monson, *See Others as They May Become*, General Conference, The Church of Jesus Christ of Latter-day Saints, Oct. 2012, Gospel Library App.

are responsible. The first comes to us in the form of incomplete science theories; the second comes to us from God.

So if agency is the key, and desire is the key to exercising agency, how do we change our desires so that we will always choose the good? The story of Alma the Younger provides an answer. As a young man, Alma the Younger was flattering the people in ways that caused them to leave the Church. After an angel appeared to him, he knew he had to repent. He asked his father for permission to go with the Sons of Mosiah and preach the gospel to the Lamanites. This was a powerful way to repent.

Alma the Younger and the sons of Mosiah had to serve. So did they go on their mission and live happily ever after? Was it easy for them to become missionaries? No. They got so discouraged at one point that they were considering returning home early. This is one of the most power- ful and instructive moments in all scripture. Their desire to serve was granted, and then they began preaching the gospel to the Lamanites and found that the work was unbelievably hard. No one was accepting their message. The people were spitting on them, running them out of town, and doing everything possible to kill their desire.

And for a brief moment—we don't know how long—their desire waned, and they wondered if they should give up and go back home. Ammon says: "Now when our hearts were depressed, and we were about to turn back, behold, the Lord comforted us, and said: Go amongst they brethren, the Lamanites, and bear with patience thine afflictions, and I will give unto you success" (Alma 26:27).

I'm taking a little liberty here, but look what happened. Their hearts became depressed. This means that their desire just got up and went. They did not want to continue. It was just too hard. They probably talked among themselves. One might have said, "This is a waste of time. We're not finding any success. We might as well go home." Ammon said, "We were about to turn back." So not just one of them, but all of them were talking about it. They became discouraged as a group.

Then something happened. The verse does not make it explicit, but we can't help but think that those dedicated missionaries prayed and asked Heavenly Father what they should do. Notice that they didn't ask for knowledge at this point. They knew the gospel was true. Their tes- timonies were strong. But they lacked the will to keep preaching. And the Lord answered them. Maybe they secretly hoped the Lord would say, "It's okay. You've done your best, and you can go back home." But He didn't. He essentially said, "You know those Lamanites who have been spitting on you and trying to kill you? Go back and try again. They'll still be spitting on you and trying to kill you, but just keep trying. Be patient. Keep trying, and I'll help you succeed."

The verse uses the word *comfort*. It says that the Lord comforted them. Well, this is a strange kind of comfort—to tell someone to go back and get spit upon and attacked. He might have said, "If you use the gift of agency that I gave you before the foundation of the world, I will make you stronger so you can do what you've been called to do. Then, when those Lamanites try to kill you, I'll help you get out of their way. I'll protect you. But you need to decide to go and do. It will be in the doing that I can bless you. If you decide to give up and go back home, how can I strengthen you?" The Lord was asking them to envision success, to see themselves achieving what they had not yet been able to achieve.

So Ammon and his brothers went back. Did the Lord strengthen them? Oh, yes! They became, perhaps, the most successful missionaries in recorded history. They brought thousands into the Church.

So we have desire and decision and then the doing. Alma and the sons of Mosiah desired to serve. When their desire waned, they decided to pray and ask God what to do. He asked them to go back and do. And he promised them blessings of strength if they would do that. The Lord always keeps His promises. They went back and experienced success.

Back to our original questions: can we change our desires? The answer is yes, if we ask. Can we change our desires on our own? The answer is no. Without divine help, we cannot change our desires. We might change our actions temporarily, but we cannot change our desires on our own. The scriptures teach that "he [meaning the Lord] changed their hearts" (Alma 5:7) so they had "no more disposition [or desire] to do evil, but to do good continually" (Mosiah 5:2). This change in disposition came through divine help.

Think of a desire you have now that you can modify in some way. Maybe you wish you had a greater desire to attend the temple, study the scriptures, or pray daily. Until your desire changes, your habits won't change. That's why in the HEART approach to compassionate imagination, the first step is to hear Him. Then, we need to envision the change. You might find it difficult to envision a change in your desire. It's easier to envision a behavior change. But the envision phase is so important. You need to imagine what it would be like, what you would feel like if your desire changed. Then you can imagine the way to help that change come about. You envision your God-given agency taking control rather than allowing any external force to overcome you. This is essential if we want to become one with God and find unity with others. We have the power within us to envision the change, and we know that God has the power to change our hearts.

Chapter 14

Avoid Cognitive Rigidity

If we want to envision ourselves changing and gradually becoming more like God, there are several things we should avoid, one of which psychologists call "cognitive rigidity." Imagination is a fluid, open-minded process. Rigidity is the opposite, and we might all fall prey to it at times.

We encounter people now and again who say, "Hey, look, it's either my way or the highway." In other words, they hold tenaciously to their position even when better alternatives are presented. They seem inflexible and immovable. And that means they are not very good team players. They like to go it alone. We might say they're not very imaginative.

Cognitive rigidity means they have difficulty changing their mind once they've stated their position. This can have obvious negative effects on relationships. When someone is cognitively rigid, they stop talking. They've made up their mind, and that's it.

Lolly: Sometimes we can be in a meeting, and the person conducting the meeting expresses a position that a group member opposes. The committee member exhibits passive-aggressive behaviors. Nothing is said at the time, and no comment is made when asked specifically—just a silent wall. The head is bowed, eyes focused downward, and lips are tight, and any further participation in the meeting is perfunctory.

Because there was no further comment offered, the decision was made without everyone's input. This differs markedly from the way our Church leaders counsel together. Usually, the presiding leader asks for input and delays his or her opinion until all have spoken, followed by further discussion or tabling of the proposal until it comes forward again. No important decision affecting the Church is made without unanimous approval. This oneness and unity come when everyone's heart totally favors the discussion item.

In marriage, cognitive rigidity can be a disaster because one of the primary indicators of good marital communication is how the couple handles conflict. When they disagree, can they keep talking with each other, try to understand the other's point of view, and remain open to a different way of doing things?

But cognitive rigidity also has implications way beyond marriage. Think of leaders, for example. Do you want to work for a leader who is open and flexible or one who is rigid and immovable? Pretty simple. The traits of cognitive rigidity and social rigidity affect us every day. Some have asked about the qualities I look for in a leader. My first response is flexibility. Rigid thinkers kill creativity, innovation, and progress. Flexible thinkers nurture these things. So if we want unity in our family, ward, neighborhood, community, and workplace, we must avoid cognitive rigidity.

Cognitive rigidity determines one's ability to solve problems. Cognitively rigid people see things only one way and have a hard time considering a differing point of view. For the cognitively rigid, uncertainty or ambiguity are hard to handle. They have a low tolerance for uncertainty. They like things to be certain, simple, and straightforward. They don't like to tackle complex problems that don't have obvious answers.

Now, let's think of socially rigid people. These people might be extremely conservative and are often xenophobic—which means they are always suspect of people from another nation or culture. They see things their way and believe that others should also see things their way. They can be susceptible to nonsensical assertions. They might subscribe to conspiracy theories. Social rigidity makes it difficult for them to form healthy relationships because they are unbending and quick to disagree.

Psychologists have studied how cognitive rigidity and social rigidity correlate. They have previously researched these two traits separately. Still, a new study looks at the effects of cognitive rigidity on social rigidity—so the study caught my eye because I am interested in how we can experience unified, healthy, and whole relationships.

The authors of the study conclude that cognitive rigidity makes it difficult for people to solve problems. The researchers noted that being a good problem solver requires the ability to overcome rigid perspectives, seek alternative reasoning paths, and tolerate ambiguity. They argued that this thinking skill is reflected in other forms of social reasoning, such as being open-minded and questioning established norms. In contrast, individuals with high social rigidity tend to be less flexible in their thinking, which hinders their problem-solving abilities.[29]

My summary of this conclusion is that rigidity hurts people. Being rigid makes it more difficult for them to solve complex problems. They are less creative, less productive, and less fulfilled. They suffer in their relationships because they are always frustrated when others see things differently. Cognitive and social rigidity, I believe, make it difficult to hear Him. They have difficulty envisioning oneness and unity. Cognitive rigidity is like putting a clamp on our brains. But to develop compassionate imagination, we need to unclamp the brain and see others as they might become.

Think of the Savior when He walked the earth. Certain people gravitated to Him, while others spurned, attacked, and eventually crucified Him. Those who accepted His teachings had to be open and flexible. His teachings were quite radical at that time. He was trying to help them get beyond the law of Moses—an eye for an eye—and help them see that they should love each other as He loved them. Radical. He taught them that the Sabbath was made for man, not man for the Sabbath—that it was okay to heal someone on the Sabbath. Radical. He tried to help them understand that He came to earth to save everyone from physical and spiritual death. Radical. And sometimes, even those who loved and revered Him as the Son of God had difficulty fully comprehending what He was teaching them.

---

29. Carola Salvi, "The Link between Cognitive and Social Rigidity," July 2023, John Cabot University.

Now we come to our day. We have living prophets, seers, and revelators—special witnesses who have been ordained and commissioned to testify of the Savior and help us, all of God's children, navigate mortality. We ask ourselves: can we be open to new revelation? Can we be flexible enough to accept a new way of thinking and doing things? Can we be totally devoted to God? This is a daily question we could ask ourselves. It's not a one-and-done decision. Every teaching that flows from those we sustain as living prophets is a new invitation. Will we respond as the Sadducees and Pharisees did? Or will we open ourselves to newness, embrace it, and live it?

These questions have so much to do with our relationship with God and with others. If we want to increase our capacity to hear the Lord's word and envision becoming like Him, we need to find ways to avoid rigidity in our thinking and behavior. We need to see with new eyes and hear with new ears, and then we need to use our agency to draw upon the Lord's grace to lift us to a new level—to feel at one with ourselves, oneness with God, and unity with others.

CHAPTER 15
OVERCOME AN ACE

I ONCE COUNSELED A YOUNG MAN WHO BECAME VERY PENSIVE AND began looking at the floor instead of looking at me as he spoke. He said:

> When I was growing up, my mother was always in bed. I never understood why. She was just always in bed when I got home from school. I had to clean the kitchen, do the breakfast dishes, and then as I got older, I had to fix dinner. I finally came to understand that she suffered from severe depression. But when I was young, I thought she was just lazy and wanted me to do all the work. While I was doing the dishes, I would look out the window and see all my friends playing frisbee or baseball, and I wished I could go play with them. But I couldn't. I resented my mother a lot. Now I understand that her disease made it impossible for her to watch over the family, but when I was young, I didn't understand that at all. I thought she just didn't care.

My friend experienced a lot of adverse childhood experiences, or ACEs. Having a parent with emotional illness is not the only kind of ACE. All types of abuse—harsh language, yelling, sexual abuse, etc. are forms of adverse childhood experiences. So too are parents with substance abuse problems or parents who have been incarcerated. These adverse experiences have a deep and lasting impact on children, an impact that can affect their entire life.

ACEs are too common. Some studies estimate that over 60% of adults have had at least one ACE, and one in seven adults have had four or more. Not surprisingly, research has also shown that ACEs lead to attachment problems in adulthood.[30] It only stands to reason that a child who does not have a safe, secure attachment to parents will have difficulty forming a safe, secure attachment to a spouse. And when attachment disorders occur, feeling oneness with God and unity in a family is impossible. Oneness can come only after we overcome the effects of rejection that ACEs bring.

ACEs not only lead to problems in family relationships, but they also raise the risk of physical disease and mental illness in adulthood. Those who have experienced multiple ACEs in childhood tend to have serious problems in adulthood, including hypertension, heart disease, diabetes, poor mental health, and premature mortality. As someone once said, "your biography can become your biology." This shows how absolutely essential it is to give children close, loving, secure relationships in their early years.

There are online quizzes you can take to assess the severity of your own ACEs. The higher the score on these quizzes, the higher the likelihood that you will have difficulties with relationships and physical health problems as an adult.

Lolly and I once heard a respected church leader say, "Remember, no one had a perfect childhood." He was urging his listeners to avoid becoming a victim and blaming all of their problems on their parents. It was wise counsel. So I recommend that you take a look at your own childhood to see if you experienced any ACEs. And if you did, how severe and frequent were they? Complete one of the online assessment instruments if you believe it would help. And then you might consider doing the following to proactively heal from your ACEs:

1) **Write about your ACE.** The simple act of writing down your ACEs can be therapeutic. Writing about your ACEs helps you articulate your own feelings at the time they occurred, just as my friend described his feelings about his depressed mother.

2) **Prayer and mindfulness.** When we turn off our devices and take time to focus on our own well-being, healing can come. As the scripture says, "Be still, and know that I am God" (Psalms

---

30. Centers for Disease Control and Prevention, Preventing Early Trauma to Improve Adult Health, 2019, https://www.cdc.gov/vitalsigns/aces/index.html#:~:text=61% of adults had at,health problems across the lifespan.

46:10). Prayer, as well as meditation, can help you move beyond past trauma.

3) Various types of therapy. If needed, you might access psychotherapy that will help you overcome the damage done by ACEs you experienced early in your life.

4) Fitness programs. Exercise is an all-around healer for emotional and physical illness. I recommend it highly.

I hope this brief chapter might help you or someone you love seek the help needed to get beyond the effects of adverse childhood experiences. One thing I know for sure: denying such experiences, pretending they didn't happen, or ignoring them does not work. I also know that with the right help, we can all overcome the negative effects of these experiences that happened in our early years. The Master Healer can help us. The Savior understands. And His arms are always open, his hands always extended. So our hope is that you will draw upon His love and the help from others as you overcome your own ACEs or help someone you love overcome theirs.

There is, perhaps, no better example of compassionate imagination than the process of overcoming adverse childhood experiences. We must imagine ourselves without the negative effects of these experiences. We must have compassion for parents and forgive them as the young man did who had a depressed mother. When he recounted his story he had no rancor, no anger toward his mother, only understanding. He showed compassion to the one he had resented as a child. Every time we extend such compassion, we draw closer to the Lord. We feel at one with ourselves and with Him.

CHAPTER 16

CONQUER INTOLERANCE OF UNCERTAINTY

FEAR GETS IN THE WAY OF COMPASSIONATE IMAGINATION. WHEN WE begin cycling through our worries and concerns, imagination and compassion can be blocked. Fear turns us toward ourselves, our pain, our frustrations, our disappointments. Compassionate imagination turns us toward God and others. Compassion is an other-faced emotion, an emotion that leads us to reach out, support, and lift others.

One of the enemies of compassionate imagination is our intolerance of uncertainty—or IU, as social scientists call it. It is another term for fear. We might also call it "anxiety disorder." And anxiety disorders are becoming an epidemic. One survey shows that 44% of college students struggle with anxiety disorder.[31] That doesn't mean that they periodically have some anxiety—it means they have an anxiety disorder. There's a difference. Everyone experiences anxiety from time to time. We worry about money. We worry about our weight. We worry about each other. That's normal, but nearly half of all college students have much more than that. They have an anxiety disorder, meaning they spend significant time every day filled with fear, which can be debilitating.

---

31. K.N. Shine, "College students' anxiety, depression higher than ever, but so are efforts to receive care," *University of Michigan News*, 2023, https://news. umich.edu/college-students-anxiety-depression-higher-than-ever-but-so-are-efforts-to-receive-care/.

Lolly: When we were senior missionaries teaching religion courses at BYU Hawaii, we had several students who had special accommodations allowed for them. Because of their diagnosed emotional illness, they were allowed extra time for test-taking, accommodation with attendance, and special tutoring. In other words, they needed special kid-glove handling in how we presented assignments. Some were successful, but even with several accommodations, some students could not stay in school because of severe depression and other mental disorders. Students and faculty were sent home in March 2020 because of COVID-19, and the pandemic only escalated these anxious feelings in students.

During the last years of teaching in public schools, I noticed a gradual increase in emotional problems that students brought to my classroom. I taught in a sixth-grade classroom, so I got to really know and understand my students during our nine months together. I soon learned that I needed to spend significant time teaching coping strategies for success. I found that my grading practices could be especially helpful for anxious students, even at the age of twelve. I taught them that if they chose to learn and tried their very best, I would devise a way for them to be successful. First, I taught them they had to have Desire, then make a Decision to do right, and then be Determined to make it happen with extra effort if needed. We called it the Three Ds of Success. We even wrote a song: "Desire, Decision, Determination, Yes! These are the three Ds, the three Ds of success."

Too many do not experience this kind of success. Nearly a third of our youth ages 13–18 have an anxiety disorder. And about the same percentage of adults suffer similarly.[32] That's a large portion of the population. That means if you approach three people, one of them could have an anxiety disorder. So I've been asking myself: what leads to anxiety? What's the precursor? If we could identify the cause of anxiety, we could likely help more people overcome the disorder.

Well, I'm not the first to ask these questions. Psychologists have been trying to figure these things out for a long time. There are several theories

---

32. "Any Anxiety Disorder," *National Institute of Mental Health*, Washington, D.C., https://www.nimh.nih.gov/health/statistics/any-anxiety-disorder.

and treatments. But here's one of the most interesting insights I think can be helpful, whether or not we have a severe problem with anxiety.

Before I describe it, I want to share a bit of history. As I went through my work life, I noticed a personal quality I liked to seek when hiring someone or asking someone to help me on a creative project. I didn't know what to call it at the time. But now, I would call it "tolerance of ambiguity." I enjoyed dealing with ambiguity—the more ill-defined the problem, the more fun it was to solve. And I liked it when I could see this in others. Because some people did not possess it, they suffered from cognitive rigidity, as discussed earlier. They wanted things to be cut and dried, straightforward, and totally logical, with easy-to-find answers. But that's not how most problems are in life, so when I was engaging in creative work, I wanted to find others who enjoyed dealing with messy, complicated issues.

Lolly: Looking back over my life, the experiences Russ and I shared as mission leaders stand out as a time filled with ambiguity and dealing with the unexpected. We enjoyed a week of spiritual uplift and training at the MTC before taking over the leadership of our mission. However, there was no way to prepare us for what we experienced in the daily routine of mission leader life. Each experience had its unique set of circumstances because each missionary was one of a kind. When dealing with the lives of young missionaries, there were several complicated issues to try to understand and help solve, whether it be spiritual, emotional, or physical. Zone conferences, interviews, and training were always on our minds. We learned early that these precious young missionaries and our seasoned senior couples were blessings granted to us to help grow the church in our mission. Learning to see these missionaries as who they were becoming was our opportunity to serve and care for them.

That mission leader experience was a great teacher for me as I began a late-in-life career as a sixth-grade teacher. I was a better teacher entering the classroom following the mission. I was filled with love and eyes of compassion for these students. When people shuddered when they learned I was teaching middle-school kids, I laughed and said, "I love this age. They get my jokes, and their hormones haven't started to rage yet." I focused on every student being successful, just like we sought ways for every missionary to succeed. It was gratifying to be directed in my teaching by the Spirit and to express love and hope for them in learning how to learn.

I learned much from being a mission leader, as did Lolly. Some of that learning led to a new understanding of how some people struggle with uncertainty. Recently, I read an article on "Intolerance of Uncertainty," abbreviated IU. This concept or theory has been around since the '90s, but it's received more attention recently as anxiety disorders continue to surge due to the changes in our culture. Researchers see IU as the "fear of the unknown," a long-recognized, deep-seated fear. They're saying that intolerance of uncertainty is not a momentary fear—it's deep-seated, and it does occur in people with or without anxiety disorder. Research has shown that IU applies to many types of anxiety disorders[33]. So to understand how to deal with these disorders, we should consider IU or intolerance of uncertainty as a contributing factor.

Here's why this is important for all of us: we all deal with uncertainty every day. We're unsure how our boss might respond to our proposal, how we will perform on a test, and whether a friend will accept our invitation. We're surrounded by uncertainty and ambiguity. They are central features of mortality. The question is: How much of a threat do we perceive a future event to be? I like the word *threat* because we could also view uncertainty as a puzzle to solve or a hurdle to jump over. But threat? That's where it becomes dicey. The minute we see the upcoming test in the same way as a hiker sees a cougar running down the trail toward him, fear—real fear—kicks in and can paralyze us. When we become paralyzed, even for the short term, we lose our ability to deal with life, and anxiety takes control.

When intolerance of uncertainty strikes, how can we deal with it effectively? And if you never experience intolerance of uncertainty, you very likely know someone who does. So how can you help them? Research shows we can help by talking ourselves out of anxious feelings.

We might tell ourselves, "I just know I'm going to do badly on my class presentation (or talk in church or my Relief Society lesson)." As

---

33. "The intolerance of uncertainty construct in the context of anxiety disorders: theoretical and practical perspectives" National Library of Medicine, 2012, https://pubmed.ncbi.nlm.nih.gov/23002938/.

soon as that kind of negative "internal chatter" (the thoughts running around in our mind, seemingly unbidden at times) starts, we must consciously stop. We could say, "Hey, wait a minute—I'm prepared. I love the topic I'm going to teach about. I will sit down right now and run through it another time." While running through it, imagine how it will go in the real setting—this time in a positive, affirmative way. Use a little self-compassion and imagination as you talk your way out of the fear.

If we talk our way into feeling afraid of the future, we can talk our way out of it by re-envisioning it, by practice, and by affirmative, positive self-chatter. The importance of envisioning reappears. We need to learn how to envision going through an uncertain event with confidence and faith rather than fear and anxiety.

Here's the prophetic counsel that can change everything—counsel that can help lift us to a whole new place in dealing with anxiety. President Nelson has promised us that we can expect miracles. That's a prophetic promise from God's living oracle. This is the most powerful way to conquer intolerance of uncertainty. Rather than expecting failure or disappointment, we can flip that around with God's help and expect His divine grace to come to our aid. And when He lends His power to ours, we can always expect miracles. They don't need to be dramatic events—simply God's hand reaching down to help us. We expect miracles when we hear Him and when we envision oneness with him and unity with others.

Lolly: One person who did not suffer from intolerance of uncertainty was my mother, Lola Hansen Sedgwick. She embraced life to the fullest, and as our neighbor once described, "Your mother was a force of nature." I couldn't have agreed more. She had several famous sayings that crown our memory of her, but two stand out to me. Mostly bedridden the last couple of years of her life, we hesitated to tell her we were thinking of going on a sabbatical to Paris for a few months. When we attempted to tell her our plans, she blurted out this memorable phrase, "Oh, live it up, live it up the Lord's way!" She seemed as excited as we were in our anticipation of our adventure.

That was the way she lived her life—with great anticipation of a great adventure. This was the way she approached her eventual passing. As we visited her often in her weakened state, she would always mention and exclaim with renewed energy and faith, "I'm getting ready for my next great adventure!" She didn't know any more about death than the rest of us, but she wanted us to know that she was preparing for it and was excited to learn how it would all play out. She was eager to face the unknown with faith. Her internal chatter, even about death, was positive. She epitomized being tolerant of the uncertainty that lay ahead for her and for us all. Mother was ready and welcoming for whatever was coming.

So when we face uncertainty, we can have the kind of rock-solid faith that Lolly's mother had. We can change negative internal chatter into positive internal chatter. We can expect a miracle. If we do, compassionate imagination will increase, oneness with God will grow, and unity with others will surely follow.

CHAPTER 17
MANAGE YOUR INNER VOICE

LOLLY'S MOTHER HAD AMAZING CONTROL OVER HER THOUGHTS. SHE seemed to fear nothing. She had a remarkable capacity to envision a bright future, no matter what lay ahead. Like Lolly's mother, we all have an inner voice that never stops. It's in the background, but it is always there, and it may not be as positive as we'd like. We drop something on the floor, and we may ask ourselves, "Why didn't I hold on to that?" If we were to count all of the negative messages we say to ourselves in one day, we would be astounded. Psychologists have counted them because psychologists like to count things, and they've found that most adults have much more negative internal chatter going on in their brains than positive internal chatter.[34] Unlike Lolly's mother, most people are much more likely to talk themselves down than to talk themselves up.

You've likely heard of Rafael Nadal, the tennis player from Spain who, at the time of writing, has been ranked number one in singles in the world for 209 weeks, has finished as the year-end number one five times, and has broken numerous records in professional tennis. In his interviews and articles about him, he talks a lot about "managing his inner voice." We've called this "internal chatter," and it often consists of

---

34. Raj Raghunathan, "How Negative Is Your 'Mental Chatter?'," *Psychology Today* (2013), https://www.psychologytoday.com/us/blog/sapient-nature/201310/how-negative-is-your-mental-chatter.

negative thoughts, while at other times, it's more positive. But there is no question that we all have thoughts in our heads all day, every day. And the goal, as the Lord says in Doctrine and Covenants 121:45, is to "let virtue garnish [your] thoughts unceasingly."

The word *garnish* is a side dish, not the central feature. You garnish a plate of roasted vegetables with parsley. The roasted vegetables are the main dish. The garnish is on the side. When we're engaged in any activity, whether we're driving a car, combing our hair, or raking leaves—the car, the hair, and the leaves are the main dish, and the thoughts rolling around in our head at the same time are the parsley—the garnish. So the Lord is telling us to watch those background thoughts because those thoughts can lead you in all directions, some good and some bad. Then He's saying that if we can control those garnishing thoughts, we will be able to exercise our faith in powerful ways. Fear and anxiety will vanish. And our confidence will grow "strong in the presence of God" (Doctrine & Covenants 121:45).

So without knowing anything about the verse in the Doctrine and Covenants, here is what Rafael Nadal says about his strategy for winning a tennis match:

> What I battle hardest to do in a tennis match is to quiet the voices in my head, to shut everything out of my mind but the contest itself and concentrate every atom of my being on the point I am playing. If I made a mistake on a previous point, forget it; should a thought of victory suggest itself, crush it.[35]

You'll notice he did not say he wanted to focus every atom of his being on the game he was playing—no, Nadal wants to focus only on the point that he is trying to win. That's focus. That's being fully present. That's thought control to the max. No garnishing thoughts—only total attention to the single point at the moment.

He goes on:

> During a match, you are in a permanent battle to fight back your everyday vulnerabilities, bottle up your human feelings. The more bottled up they are, the greater your chances of winning, so long as you've trained as hard as you play, and the gap in talent is not too wide between you and your rival. The gap in talent with Federer

---

35. Haikal Kushahrin, *Rafa: My Story*—Book Summary (2021), 1, https://haikal.blog/rafa/.

existed, but it was not impossibly wide. It was narrow enough, even on his favorite surface in the tournament he played best, for me to know that if I silenced doubts and fears, and exaggerated hope, inside my head better than he did, I could beat him. You have to cage yourself in protective armor, turn yourself into a bloodless warrior. It's kind of self-hypnosis, a game you play, with deadly seriousness, to disguise you own weakness from yourself, as well as from your rival.[36]

Nadal's idea of silencing doubts and fears sounds like "Doubt not, fear not" (Doctrine & Covenants 6:36). If you think about it, doubts and fears are nothing more than garnishment to the task before us. If our task is to take a physics test, we need to silence background thoughts like, "I should have studied more, I'm so bad at taking tests," etc. And the more we let those thoughts take over even a tiny part of our brain, the more fear builds up, the more we doubt that we will pass the test.

The last sentence of the quote is important: "It's kind of self-hypnosis, a game you play, with deadly seriousness, to disguise your weakness from yourself, as well as from your rival." How do we disguise our weaknesses from ourselves? It's easy for us to imagine how a tennis player might look intentionally tough so that he can psych out his rival. But how do we disguise our weakness from ourselves? Rafael answers this for himself— he "[exaggerates] hopes." He envisions hopefulness. To me, this goes far beyond a tennis game. It is the heart of the gospel.

When negative thoughts creep onto the back burner of our brain, we need to repel those thoughts with thoughts of hope. And where does that hope come from? As the Book of Mormon says, "And what is it that ye shall hope for? Behold I say unto you that ye shall have hope through the atonement of Christ" (Moroni 7:41). He is our hope. He is the one who can quell those negative thoughts. He can fill us with his light and love, and the outcome will be much more important than winning a tennis match; it will be winning the game of life. It will be conquering our fears and gaining victory over ourselves. Then, truly will "[our] confidence wax strong in the presence of God; and the doctrine of the priesthood shall distil upon [our souls] as the dews from heaven" (Doctrine and Covenants 121:45).

Negative internal chatter is an enemy to becoming one with God and developing Christlike unity with others. It blocks our positive,

---

36. Ibid.

faith-filled actions. As President Nelson has taught, it stops our spiritual momentum.[37] We may never play in a championship tennis game, but we are playing every day in the game of life, the game of mortality—and mortality has its problems. We can talk our way out of solving those problems, or we can talk our way into solving those problems. It's all about managing our inner voice and listening to the Spirit rather than the world. Managing our inner voice is essential to envisioning oneness with God and with others.

---

37. Russell M. Nelson, *The Power of Spiritual Momentum*, General Conference, The Church of Jesus Christ of Latter-day Saints, Apr. 2022, Gospel Library App.

CHAPTER 18
DON'T BE A VICTIM

WHEN CHRIST WAS ON THE EARTH, HE TRIED TO HELP THOSE WHO would listen to forget their differences, give up their prejudice, and unite as one. His parables, preaching, and miracles all carried compassionate imagination as a foundational message. Jesus spoke to the woman at the well with compassion even though she was a Samaritan, and He was a Jew. He lived what He taught in the parable of the Good Samaritan, a story that has much to teach us about oneness and Christlike unity.

We all know that the Samaritans did not get along with the Jews, but the roots of their hatred toward each other ran far deeper than simply not getting along. They despised each other. The Samaritans had slowed the rebuilding of Jerusalem, and in about 111 BC, the Jews destroyed the Samaritan temple and ravaged the territory where the Samaritans lived.[38] Think of the Israeli-Palestinian conflict today. The rift between the Samaritans and Jews was every bit as strong as the modern-day conflict today.

When Jesus was asked who we should consider our neighbors, he told the story of the Good Samaritan. The message? Everyone is your neighbor—even your archenemy. It's the same message repeated in the April 2023 general conference: don't just love your friends; love your enemies—end contention. Eliminate conflict of any kind between individuals and groups.

---

38. Jonathan Bourgel, "The Destruction of the Samaritan Temple by John Hyrcanus: A Reconsideration," 2016, https://www.jstor.org/stable/10.15699/jbl.1353.2016.3129.

On April 13, 2023, President Nelson received the first Gandhi-King-Mandela Peace Prize in the Martin Luther King International Chapel on the campus of Morehouse College, a historically black school in Atlanta, GA. President Nelson was selected to receive the award because of his groundbreaking work in creating a partnership between the Church and the NAACP. In the words of those who oversee the award: "President Nelson was selected because of his global efforts in abandoning attitudes and actions of prejudice against any group of God's children through non-violent ways."[39]

I do not believe it is a stretch to see President Nelson as the Good Samaritan, and I think it is quite remarkable that the awards committee would select a white person to be the first recipient of an award named after an Indian, an African American, and an African. The Good Samaritan not only noticed the wounded Jew but also paid for his lodging so he could recover from his injuries. Like the Good Samaritan, President Nelson recognized NAACP members as his brothers and sisters and offered millions of dollars to help black students pursue their educational goals.

When President Nelson urges us to end contention, he's serious about it—so serious that he does all he can to show how we can do away with contention between races. Lolly and I were teenagers during the 1960s when racism in America was raging. We had a hard time understanding it then, and we still have difficulty understanding why one person would hate another simply because of their skin color.

You might remember the racist conflict in Charlottesville, Virginia, on April 11 and 12, 2017. Many city residents wanted to remove the Confederate statue of Robert E. Lee, so white supremacists staged a march to protest the statue's removal. During the march, one person was killed and 35 injured when one of the protestors rammed a car into the crowd.[40] I must admit that when people do senseless things like this, I am left wondering. What is their motive? What did marchers think they would accomplish by their protest? Was it all because of a statue? I don't believe so.

39. "The Prophet Receives the Gandhi-King-Mandela Peace Prize," *Church News*, 13 April 2023, https://newsroom.churchofjesuschrist.org/article/the-prophet-receives-gandhi-king-mandela-peace-prize.

40. Charlottesville car attack, Wikipedia, https://en.m.wikipedia.org/wiki/Charlottesville_car_attack#:~:text=The%20Charlottesville%20car%20attack%20was,one%20person%20and%20injuring%2035.

When hate develops between two groups—whether it's the Lamanites and Nephites, the Israelis and Palestinians, the Samaritans and Jews, or the Blacks and Whites—something else underlies their attitudes and actions. The protesting group during the Charlottesville tragedy—in this case, the white supremacists—fell prey to the victim mentality.

As they marched in Charlottesville, the mob's rallying cry was, "You will not replace us, you will not replace us!"[41] Who's replacing who? The white supremacists believe that Blacks and others are getting too much privilege in our society. They believe Blacks steal away opportunities from Whites in education, employment, and more. This attitude is ironic since data clearly show that Whites are still greatly advantaged compared to their black counterparts. But when anyone or any group begins to believe that another group has victimized them, they lash out at the other group, and dangerous marches occur, like the one in Charlottesville.

When we see ourselves as victims, we might begin to attribute everything that happens to us as coming from outward forces. We feel hemmed in, put upon, restricted, ignored. Our capacity to exercise our agency is diminished. Our locus of control is centered on outward forces.

In stark contrast to this interracial conflict, we read about a Samaritan man who has so much compassion for a fellow human being—even though he was a member of an enemy group—that he simply could not pass by. He had to kneel down, examine the man's wounds, do all he could to help him, and then heft him onto his donkey, transport him to an inn, and pay for his lodging so his Jewish "friend" could fully recover.

The Good Samaritan exemplifies the heart of Christianity—compassion, service, sacrifice. Every time President Nelson urges us to be kind to everyone regardless of race, gender, abilities, or any other defining attribute, his message is clear: We must treat everyone the same. They are all our brothers and sisters. We must never allow differences of opinion to separate us, and we must never ignore anyone because they are not like us. Inclusion. Belonging. These are the principles Christ taught when he was here on the earth. We are all included, and we all belong because we are all children of the same God.

Back in the '70s, while I was serving on the faculty of the National Technical Institute for the Deaf in the Rochester Institute of Technology, the associate dean for students at Stony Brook University on Long Island asked if I would consult with him on a project. I gladly accepted and flew

41. Ibid.

to Stony Brook to meet with him. He had grown up in Harlem, eventually obtained a PhD, and was trying to help students from Harlem succeed at Stony Brook, a highly competitive university. We had been talking for about an hour when he stopped the conversation and said, "Okay, I've got a question. Have you ever worked with a black person before?" My first thought was, how did he know? I shook my head, "No." He said, "I didn't think so." I then asked, "But how did you know?" He answered, "It was easy. You're trying to be too careful so you don't offend me."

That was a powerful moment for me. My friend wanted me to talk to him like I would talk to anyone else without considering his race or background in Harlem. As time passed, we developed a rich and rewarding friendship. I learned a lot from him, and I hope he learned something from me. Race faded away and was replaced with goodwill. Yes, we were both members of groups that had attacked each other. But that didn't mean we had to assume those same prejudices. We were trying to be good Samaritans to each other. And it worked.

The parable of the Good Samaritan is for us today. It's a parable of caring compassion—of universal brotherhood and sisterhood. It is a strong counter-message to the protest in Charlottesville and so many of the recent racial conflicts we've experienced in the US. It teaches us to eliminate feelings of being victimized. If the Samaritan saw the wounded Jew as someone who had robbed him of privilege—someone who had replaced him or taken something away from him—he would not have stopped to help him. But the Samaritan did not suffer from victimhood. He saw the Jewish man as a brother, not as an enemy. They were both figuratively traveling along the path of life and were both children of God. One needed help, and the other could give that help.

My constant hope is that we can follow in the footsteps of the Good Samaritan, that we can see one other as fellow humans on the path of life, and reach out to one another as President Nelson is reaching out. This is not difficult. We can all see each other as children of God, which means we need to envision them as children of God. We can all use compassionate imagination as the Good Samaritan did.

Chapter 19
Embrace Anticipation

One role of imagination is to envision the future. We can look forward to being with each other, attending a game or performance together, traveling to a new place, or gathering for a Thanksgiving feast with our family. An excitement often precedes the event, but that excitement occurs in our mind. We imagine the fun we'll have at the family reunion, the joy that we'll feel just being together.

Of all that COVID stole from us, one of its most damaging effects was the privilege of anticipating future events. During the pandemic, we could not look forward to family gatherings, sporting events, travel, performances, graduation ceremonies—we could not even look forward to attending church meetings or worshiping in the temple. Many of us felt cheated and short-changed. The events that had been integral to our lives were suddenly stripped away. Missing the events was painful, but we were also denied the privilege of anticipating the events—the excitement that precedes the gathering, the celebration, or the worship. In some ways, the pandemic temporarily crushed our compassionate imagination. How could we reach out to the others in love when we could not get together?

During the pandemic, many could look forward to receiving a package on our doorstep from Amazon. Some could still purchase a new car or a new home. We were not denied the opportunity of anticipating the arrival of new material goods, but we could not look forward to experiential events. So, looking forward to an event is often much more appealing than anticipating the arrival of a product. OK, so what does that mean?

In simple terms, it means that looking forward to the trip we took with our family to Israel brought us much more happiness than looking forward to buying new appliances for our kitchen. The Israel trip was an experiential purchase; the appliances were a purchase of material goods.

The researchers don't try to give all the reasons that the anticipation of an event brings more happiness than the anticipation of purchasing material goods. So I will give my interpretation. Before I do, I want to share my conversation with my brother Von. He told me that he and a friend, whom I will call Paul, had just purchased tickets to attend an NFL football game. Von had never attended a professional football game, and when Paul invited him to go with him to the game, he hesitated because of the cost. Let's just say the cheapest seats were not cheap! Not to mention travel and lodging costs that would accompany the ticket purchase. So Von had to think about it for a while. After deciding to accept the invitation, he called Paul to tell him. In my brother's words, "You can't believe how excited Paul was, and this guy has suffered from serious depression for a long time. He came to life when I told him I'd decided to go to the game. And then he called me back the next week to tell me all his plans for the trip—that there would be a few stopovers on the way. He was so excited; I couldn't believe it."

Why was Paul so excited? I do not believe that his excitement came from the football game itself. The event was secondary. What brought Paul joy was the anticipation of being with Von, a lifelong friend. And even though the event was months away, the happiness that comes with anticipation was even more meaningful than the football game. It's about relationships. A wise mentor of ours once said, "We were meant to love people, not things." Sometimes, people say, "I just love my new home, car, and robot vacuum." But love is a reciprocal emotion; it is an emotion we give and receive. And a home or a car or a robot cannot love you back. I believe Paul was so excited about the football game because he knew he would be with a friend who cared about him.

Anticipation has a lot to do with hope. Hope is an emotion that aims toward the future. Hope requires imagination. We can hope that something happens in the future. We can hope this problem gets solved. We can anticipate when we can put a current problem behind us and when we will heal from an injury or a disease. Anticipation can be filled with excitement as Paul and Von were for the football game. But anticipation can also be filled with the anxiety of the unknown. A couple can be filled with excitement for their upcoming marriage, but they can also be overcome at moments with the anxiety that comes with such a permanent decision. They hope everything will turn out how they want, but they get anxious that something might go wrong. So embracing anticipation means embracing all of it—the unknown aspect that can bring anxiety and the known aspect that can bring positive excitement. We need to imagine the future in positive ways.

Thank goodness the pandemic ended. I'm so grateful that we can look forward to future events—especially being together with those we love. Lolly and I will probably still track an Amazon package we're looking forward to receiving but recognize that the package will not bring happiness. That package cannot love us back. But our family and friends can.

Lolly: When we visited the Western Wall or Wailing Wall in Jerusalem with our adult children and spouses, it was the Jewish Sabbath, and the square was filled with throngs of pilgrims. At this sacred religious site, our guide encouraged us to join those praying at the wall. He invited us to engage in conversation if they were willing. Men and women were divided at the wall, never turning their backs as they depart from the wall. We observed happy and joyous Jews praying, singing, and dancing. Yes, dancing! We all came away with the same impression. They understand what it means to "make the Sabbath a delight."[42] In discussing our experiences there, we all became more determined to make our Sabbaths more joyful and celebratory in our Sunday worship at home and at church. I believe this joy and celebration should also carry over into our temple worship. The Jews anticipate weekly their Sabbath celebration. I want to look forward to my Sabbath day activities and temple worship with that same hopeful expectation. Can we all look forward with a little more faith that things will turn out for the best with joyful anticipation? They even bid each other a peaceful Sabbath by greeting each other with "Shabbat Shalom!"

When the scriptures say that we should delight in the Sabbath, the Jews exemplify the word *delight* better than anyone we've ever seen. They not only look forward to and anticipate the Sabbath with great joy, but

---

42. Russell M. Nelson, *The Sabbath Is a Delight*, General Conference, The Church of Jesus Christ of Latter-day Saints, Apr. 2015, Gospel Library App.

they celebrate it, too—not like a birthday, but a celebration of their love of God. We could ask ourselves: do we look forward to the Sabbath as much as the Jews we witnessed at the Western Wall do, and do our children and grandchildren? We invite you to reflect on your Sabbath Day worship and embrace the anticipation of making the Sabbath Day a delight!

The HEART Approach—A: Act in Faith

IN THE HEART APPROACH TO COMPASSIONATE IMAGINATION, WE OPEN ourselves to personal revelation, we hear Him, we envision oneness and Christlike unity, and we act in faith. When we act in faith, we are motivated by our love for the Savior. The fourth article of faith teaches us that the first principle of the gospel is not faith; it's "faith in the Lord Jesus Christ." So any time we act in faith, we are doing what God wants us to do. We are patterning ourselves after Him. It's not acting with a positive outlook, as motivational speakers might describe it. Acting in faith is much more than that. It's turning our will to God and doing what he would have us do at each moment.

Acting in faith leads to optimism. I find it so reassuring that living prophets are consistently optimistic. They are keenly aware of the problems in the world and in the Church, but their optimism seems never to falter. President Nelson is the epitome of optimism, and so was President Hinckley. Here's a taste of his optimism:

> We have every reason to be optimistic in this world. Tragedy is around, yes. Problems everywhere, yes. But . . . you can't, you don't, build out of pessimism or cynicism. You look with optimism, work with faith, and things happen.
>
> Do not despair. Do not give up. Look for the sunlight through the clouds. Opportunities will eventually open to you. Do not let the prophets of gloom endanger your possibilities.[43]

---

43. *Teachings of Presidents of the Church: Gordon B. Hinckley* (Salt Lake City: The Church of Jesus Christ of Latter-day Saints, 2016), p.71.

Optimism is not synonymous with faith; it is a prerequisite to exercising faith. The more optimistic you become, the more you want to exercise your faith to reach your goal. Remember, the first principle of the gospel is faith in the Lord Jesus Christ. Faith in his power to forgive. Faith in his power to strengthen. Optimism leads you to act in faith because you believe something that first seemed impossible can occur. Faith in the Lord gives you the strength to imagine it and accomplish it. This kind of faith, undergirded by optimism, is essential to compassionate imagination. Optimism requires imagination. Those who are optimistic see the future with brightness and hope. That is why hope is magnified by compassionate imagination. Acting in faith and optimism are reciprocal; they feed each other. The more we act in faith, the more optimistic we become, and the more optimistic we become, the more we are compelled to act in faith to reach the imagined outcome.

It's important to discuss how faith leads to action, how we can increase our faith, and how we can ensure that we follow God's will. We all want to "act and not be acted upon." But we live in a world that tries to act upon us daily. News media, fashion trends, eating fads—so many forces frequently try to act upon us without us even recognizing it. Our task is to recognize and resist the conspiring forces around us. Acting in faith is not as simple as it may appear. And when we're unsure of the next step we should take, acting in faith becomes even more challenging. God is on our side. He's always on our side. But we must let Him in. Faith in Jesus Christ is a divine power that becomes our personal strength. The more faith we have in the one who gave us life, the more life He can give us.

CHAPTER 20

GIVE YOURSELF THE GIFT OF FAITH

DURING CHRISTMAS, WE NATURALLY THINK OF ALL THE GIFTS WE CAN give others. But one gift we could think about giving ourselves is the gift of faith. And the only way we can receive that gift is to open ourselves to God. Faith, after all, is a spiritual gift. It's not a physical or an intellectual talent. It's a gift of the Spirit. And we likely already have a certain amount of faith, so the real question is: How can we build upon our current gift? How can we increase our faith?

President Hinckley once said that he viewed an increase of faith as our most important need. His talk was not only a plea; it was a prayer. He prayed to God during his talk that we could increase our faith. In his words: "Lord, increase our faith in one another, and in ourselves, and in our capacity to do good and great things. [44] Most of us try to do "good" things, but President Hinckley was praying that we would do "great" things. He was helping us understand what it meant to act in faith.

When President Kimball was called as a member of the Twelve, he knew he'd been called to do great things, but he felt inadequate. He even questioned whether the call was inspired. In the words of his sons, who wrote his biography, "How I prayed! he recalled. How I suffered! How I wept! How I struggled! As he agonized, a dream came to him of his

---

44. Gordon B. Hinckley, *"Lord, Increase Our Faith,"* General Conference, The Church of Jesus Christ of Latter-day Saints, Oct. 1987, Gospel Library App.

grandfather Heber C. Kimball and 'the great work he had done.' A calm feeling of assurance came over me, doubt and questionings subdued."[45]

This is a dramatic example of what President Hinckley was talking about. President Kimball could not see himself as a member of the Twelve. It was too daunting. It looked impossible, so impossible that he began to cry uncontrollably. But the Lord increased his faith through a dream-vision of his grandfather. That experience with his grandfather was a gift from God, a form of personal revelation because that is how faith is increased. And we can all receive that gift even if our experience is not quite as dramatic as President Kimball's.

Many years ago, when I was serving in a bishopric, I visited with a sister in the ward and extended a call for her to serve in the Young Women. She was surprised, maybe not as stunned as President Kimball had been, but very surprised nonetheless. She spoke with pain and hesitancy as if pleading for the call to not be extended: "I've never served in Young Women before. I've always served in the Primary. I just don't know if I can do it." She accepted the call and served well. The Lord increased her faith to accomplish the task He had given her.

We all need the gift of faith because we sometimes worry that we will fail. The task seems too difficult, too scary. Nelson Mandela sat in jail for twenty-seven years before becoming one of the world's most revered leaders. Twenty-seven years! But even with all the adversity he experienced, he once said, "I never lose; I either win or learn."[46]

I love this mantra. It's what faith is all about. His quote means that no matter how scary the task is ahead of you, you don't need to worry about failing or losing; you just need to learn from experience that you can succeed. And even though he did not refer to God, I believe that the way you learn that you can do whatever you have been called to do is by relying on the Lord's grace to strengthen you. God is eager to give each of us this gift of faith.

In Elder Lance Wickman's conference talk, "But If Not," he refers to the story in the book of Daniel when Shadrach, Meshach, and Abednego

45. Edward L. Kimball and Andrew E. Kimball, *Spencer W. Kimball, Twelfth President of the Church of Jesus Christ of Latter-day Saints* (Salt Lake City: Bookcraft, 1977), p.19.
46. Philippe AIMÉ, "How to win or learn like Nelson Mandela, rather than simply repeating mistakes," Medium, 13 March 2017, https://medium.com/@philippeAIME/how-to-win-or-learn-like-nelson-mandela-rather-than-simply-repeating-mistakes-2b4c45e33078.

were thrown into the fiery furnace because they would not bow down to the King's image.

The three Hebrew magistrates expressed trust that the Lord would deliver them from the fiery furnace, *"but if not,"* they said to the king, "we [still] will not serve thy gods (Daniel 3:18; emphasis added). Significantly, not three but four men were seen in the midst of the flames, and "the form of the fourth [was] like the Son of God" (Daniel 3:25).[47]

Two important insights from this story: 1) no matter the outcome—even if the flames devoured them—they would not renounce their faith in God, and 2) the Lord intervened and preserved them. They did not lose the battle. They did not fail. All because they exercised faith in God.

Shadrach, Meshach, and Abednego knew the Lord. They drew close to Him throughout their lives, and He drew close to them. And their faith allowed them to act—to enter the fiery furnace even though it was scary. The main message in this chapter is that we need to act—to exercise our faith, because faith is a principle of action. Our faith will not increase if we remain passively on the sidelines watching everyone else. We've got to jump in and enter the fray ourselves.

Chad Webb, a Church educator, once said: "Joseph Smith taught that exercising faith in God requires us to have 'a correct idea of his character, perfections, and attributes' and a 'knowledge that the course of life which [we are] pursuing is according to his will.' Both of these imperatives require us to exercise faith as a principle of action."[48]

We all need to know that our path is the one God wants us to follow. When Moroni told the young prophet Joseph that God had a work for him to do, Joseph could have said, "Well, that's too scary. I don't think I can do that. I'm too young. I don't know enough." But he didn't say that. He jumped in. He acted. And then he relied on the Lord to increase his faith. And the persecution he experienced was at least as scary as the fiery furnace that Shadrach, Meshach, and Abednego jumped into.

---

47. Lance B. Wickman, *But If Not*, General Conference, The Church of Jesus Christ of Latter-day Saints, Oct. 2002, Gospel Library App.
48. Chad H. Webb, "Faith as a Principle of Action and Power," *Ensign*, 13 June 2017, https://www.churchofjesuschrist.org/broadcasts/article/satellite-training-broadcast/2017/06/faith-as-a-principle-of-action-and-power?lang=eng.

So to receive the gift of faith that the Lord is so eager to give us, we need to take a step into the unknown, and if we're on the path the Lord has asked us to follow, He will surely come to our aid.

Years ago, Lolly and I composed the words and music to a Christmas song, "He Brought New Light." She and I love to hear our granddaughters sing this, blending in harmony.

> He brought new light that Christmas Day,
> He brought new light to show the way,
> He brought new hope; he brought new love,
> The Son of God from heav'n above.
> He brought new peace upon the earth,
> A change of heart of priceless worth,
> He brought new joy that Christmas night,
> He brought new light.

What does that light bring us? It brings us the power to act, think a new thought, find a new solution, create a new path, and develop a new skill—all of which require compassionate imagination. It is His light we seek, and the more we seek it, the more faith we will have to face whatever comes our way. But to receive His light, we need to act and attempt what may seem impossible, just as President Kimball accepted his call to the Twelve or as my friend accepted her call to serve the Young Women of her ward.

If we don't succeed immediately, we have not failed; we have learned something we did not understand before, like Nelson Mandela said. We don't get discouraged because of what might seem like a failed attempt. We adjust, imagine a new approach, and try again. Because if it is something God wants us to do—and that is the important thing—then we know He will make it possible for us to achieve it. This is not about self-confidence, self-esteem, or self-actualization. It's about having faith, real faith, in the One who can empower us to accomplish whatever He wants us to accomplish. We focus on God rather than on our weaknesses.

With this focus, we can all experience an increase of faith, as President Hinckley prayed for: Faith in the Lord, faith in one another, and faith in ourselves that we can do good and great things. That kind of faith requires compassionate imagination. We need to imagine ourselves doing those good and great things. We need to know that the Lord will help us out of his compassion for us, His children.

CHAPTER 21
GET YOUR HEART RIGHT

ONE ASPECT OF COMPASSIONATE IMAGINATION IS GETTING OUR HEART right. It's a matter of tuning ourselves to the Lord. Our granddaughter shared a thought with us that has real merit. She is currently serving a mission and was concerned that missionaries can sometimes attribute success in missionary work to the missionaries alone. She said, "Well, if you go hear a great piano concert, you don't say: 'Wow, that's a great piano!' The praise goes to the one who is playing the piano. It's the same with the missionaries. The Lord is the musician; I'm just the instrument. He's the one we praise, not the missionary."

In the eighth chapter of Acts, we read about a man named Simon who wanted to be able to lay his hands on others and give them the gift of the Holy Ghost, as he had seen the apostles do. So he offered Peter money to get this power. You can imagine Peter's dismay at such a request. Why would this man think that Priesthood power could be purchased? Likely because this man was accustomed to getting whatever he wanted by offering money. But Peter's rebuke is meaningful for all of us, whether or not we would ever think of purchasing a gift from God.

> Thou hast neither part nor lot in this matter: for thy heart is not right in the sight of God. Repent therefore of this thy wickedness, and pray God, if perhaps the thought of thine heart may be forgiven thee (Acts 8:21–22).

We know God looks on the heart much more than the outward appearance. Simon had wanted to do something good by bestowing the

Holy Ghost on others, but he apparently wanted that power for the wrong reason, perhaps so that others would honor and respect him. Taking it one step further, if he had been given power to bestow the Holy Ghost and had done it to be "seen of men," he would have been committing an evil act.

I once had a conversation on this topic with a member of the Church who had difficulty seeing why it was so important to have pure intent. I asked, "So what if a person pays tithing grudgingly? She said, "Well, that's better than not paying it at all." So then we read together in the seventh chapter of Moroni:

> For I remember the word of God which saith by their works ye shall know them; for if their works be good, then they are good also. For behold, God hath said a man being evil cannot do that which is good; for if he offereth a gift, or prayeth unto God, except he shall do it with real intent it profiteth him nothing. For behold, it is not counted unto him for righteousness. For behold, if a man being evil giveth a gift, he doeth it grudgingly; wherefore it is counted unto him the same as if he had retained the gift, wherefore he is counted evil before God (Moroni 7:5–8).

Lolly: Through the years, we've spent some time in French-speaking countries, so we've tried to supplement my high school French at various times by reading the French scriptures alongside English scriptures in hopes that something might sink in. Aside from learning new French words, we've found this study enhances our meaning of the scriptures in English. One day we came across the French word *contrecœur*, which means "against heart." This is the translation for the word *grudgingly*. What an apt description of what it means to do something grudgingly. You're going against yourself; your desires don't match what you signed up to do. For example, maybe the assignment sheet for cleaning the church is empty, so you feel like you should put your name down, but deep down inside, you don't want to. Doing things halfheartedly or without really wanting to is harmful. Doing things for the wrong reasons is never right. We've got to do the right thing for the right reason.

So does that mean we don't need to do something when we don't feel like doing it? What if someone asks us to substitute in Primary at the last minute, and we don't feel like doing it? We know it would be wrong to do it against our will because we don't like it, so we refuse the invitation. This gets complicated. We could say, "Since I don't feel like doing it, I shouldn't do it because my heart would not be in it."

This is what we call "cognitive dissonance." Cognitive dissonance is "the state of having inconsistent thoughts, beliefs, or attitudes, especially relating to behavioral decision and attitude change." We're right back to *contrecœur*—going against our own heart, our own desires. Cognitive dissonance occurs when we have a sort of internal battle within us. A part of us wants to do something, but another part of us wants not to do it.

Ministering might be one example. We might say, "I know I should visit my families, but I don't feel like it right now. Maybe I'll send a text instead." We know our lack of desire is not good, so we need to keep rethinking it to overcome the cognitive dissonance. If we do it grudgingly, neither we nor the person we visit will be blessed. We should do it wholeheartedly or not at all. So we need a change of heart. This is so central to compassionate imagination. When we experience cognitive dissonance, one solution is to imagine our way out of it. We need to imagine ourselves as being compassionate. This is somewhat like William James, who believed that if we want to acquire a certain trait, we should act as if we already have it, and the trait will eventually become part of us.[49]

Being reluctant to do what we know we should do can cause internal conflict, but so can temptations. I once interviewed a 14-year-old boy who liked to steal cars. He said, "Well, when I see a car with the key in the ignition, I just gotta steal it, just take it for a ride. I can't stop myself." So I kept asking him how he was planning to overcome this desire. He said, "I kinda have a conversation with myself. I say, I wanna take it, but I know it's wrong. So I just keep saying this until I can walk away and leave the car alone."

One thing we know for certain: if we're going to experience a change of heart, we need God's help. We cannot change our own heart. If we want to get our heart right, we need to exercise compassionate imagination.

---

49   William James, Brainy Quotes—Famous Quotes, https://www.brainyquote.com/quotes/william_james_163787.

So the next time you experience cognitive dissonance and have one of those conversations inside your head, consider calling upon the powers of heaven to help you. Consider imagining your way out of the internal conflict. Be compassionate with yourself as you make the change. Know that the Lord will help you make the change because you genuinely try to do His will, whether you're thinking of giving up an undesirable behavior or putting your whole heart into something you've done half-heartedly. I truly believe that by opening yourself to God's compassion and feeling compassion for yourself, you can get your heart right.

Chapter 22

Exercise Collective Faith

Of all the topics that could be discussed in this book, Christlike unity is at the top of the list. You may wonder why I use the words *oneness* and *unity* in the book. Doesn't oneness include unity? Yes, in a way, it does. But I think both words are helpful as we try to establish Zion. Unity connotes togetherness—when people with different backgrounds join together in one organization. A family can experience unity. A ward can experience unity. I like to use the word *oneness* as the relationship we seek with God. Our goal should be to be completely one with God. But we should also want to be unified with one another. We may still disagree on unimportant matters, but we are unified in our faith and our aspiration for eternal life.

Paul was concerned about the disunity among the people of Corinth, so he counseled them quite directly: "Now I beseech you, brethren, by the name of our Lord Jesus Christ, that ye all speak the same thing, and that there be no divisions among you; but that ye be perfectly joined together in the same mind and in the same judgment" (1 Corinthians 1:10).

Some wonder if the scriptures in the New Testament are still relevant in today's world. I believe everyone would agree that Paul's counsel to the Corinthians way back in 53 AD is extremely relevant to our lives today.

President Nelson's talk on being peacemakers is the same message Paul delivered 2,000 years ago.

President Nelson's counsel, I'm sure, was inspired by the divisiveness we are now experiencing in our world. And he did not spare us as members of the Church. He got a nice chuckle from the audience when he said,

> At this point you may be thinking that this message would really help someone you know. Perhaps you are hoping that it will help him or her to be nicer to you. I hope it will! But I also hope that you will look deeply into *your* heart to see if there are shards of pride or jealousy that prevent *you* from becoming a peacemaker.[50]

Paul didn't use the word *peacemaker*, but when he said we need to be "perfectly joined together," he said precisely the same thing President Nelson was teaching us.

So to be unified does not mean we need to think exactly like someone else or agree with others all the time. I know a couple who see things quite differently. One is a Democrat, the other Republican. They vote for different candidates in any election. But they are united as a couple. They disagree about certain political matters but are still extremely supportive of each other and unified in their marriage relationship. Their faith is the same. Their ultimate goals are the same. And I believe they have compassion toward each other on their differences.

I like the term "collective faith." It's not used very often in our church, but it describes what Paul was teaching with the word *unity* and what President Nelson was teaching us about eliminating contention.

Think of the image of a family combining their faith on behalf of a family member suffering from a disease or serving a mission. Each family member exercises faith individually, combining their faith as they pray for the same purpose. They form a collective or combined faith.

When we join together, we can call down the powers of heaven more effectively than when we act in isolation. President Nelson wants us to be peacemakers together. Peacemaking is, by definition, a communal activity, not an individual activity. We can envision, for example, the married couple I mentioned praying together that effective leaders will be elected

---

50. Russell M. Nelson, *Peacemakers Needed*, General Conference, The Church of Jesus Christ of Latter-day Saints, Apr. 2023, Gospel Library App.

to guide our country through a difficult time. After combining their faith, they might still vote for two different qualified candidates.

So families can exercise collective faith, but ward members can also exercise collective faith on behalf of a ward member or our country. When we join together in faith, our actions become more purposeful and more meaningful. I remember watching approximately 75 young single adults provide disaster relief for those whose homes had been flooded following a torrential downpour.

We visited a home where the owner was standing on her balcony as she watched these young people tear out damaged sheetrock from her home and pile it at the curb so that it would be picked up by trucks circulating through the neighborhoods. She saw us below her balcony and called, "Hey, please wait; I want to say something to you. I'm not a member of your church, but I understand that you came from Salt Lake today. When you return to Salt Lake, I want you to tell your church leaders how grateful I am for the help these young people have given me. I don't know what we would have done without them. Even though I'm not a member, I think your church is the best in the world."

She did say that. And I believe that she was also saying that it was the collective action of the youth that impressed her—all working together toward the same goal—to relieve suffering following a natural disaster. But the collective action required collective faith. Everyone involved was praying that they would be able to give the help that was needed. They were united in their faith. This is a central principle of the restored Gospel and the core idea of compassionate imagination. If some youth were fighting against the project and in constant opposition to the goal or playing around instead of working, nothing good would have been accomplished.

This is what Paul and President Nelson have taught us. Exercise collective faith. Join with others. Work together. It applies to missionary companions, married couples, siblings, and co-workers, that all may come to a Christlike unity of the faith.

I can't think of a more important message right now in our culture. We are experiencing an unprecedented form of toxicity in civil discourse. We seem unable to discuss any issue without taking sides and verbally attacking each other. This is the opposite of peacemaking, harming our nation and neighborhoods. So we dream that we can learn to exercise collective faith, come together on the issues that matter most, and value our relationships with one another more than we value the position we take on a certain issue. That means that we need to understand each other better, that we need to learn to see things from the other point of view, and that we need to be open to modifying our position when we learn something new that helps us see things in a new and different way.

As God's children, we should pray for Christlike unity. Certainly, that is what the people did in the time of Enoch. They were so concerned about the welfare of their neighbor that they did not let differences of opinion damage their relationship. They placed God first. They loved God first and foremost, leading them to love one another, so the differences that once may have divided them disappeared. The scales that covered their eyes fell away, and they began to see things clearly as God saw them.

So we could pray, as did Paul, that we "be perfectly joined together in the same mind." This kind of Christlike unity requires imagination—not just any kind of imagination, but compassionate imagination—born out of love for God and for each other. Can we envision a unified nation or world? Conflicts keep festering everywhere. But the central purpose of the gospel of Jesus Christ is to help us overcome conflict, join together in love, and serve one another. Compassionate imagination is the way to create oneness with God and Christlike unity with all His children.

CHAPTER 23
TAKE UP YOUR CROSS

WHEN WE ACT IN FAITH, WE RESIST THE INFLUENCES THAT WOULD move us away from the Savior. We draw upon His grace to overcome the distractions that we constantly face. The challenge is that we live in a world that plays to our selfishness. Think of the ads on TV. The ad designers do everything possible to make their products appear irresistible. They even use words like *crave* to convince you that you cannot live without the pizza with cheese on the top and cheese on the bottom and cheese inside the crust, or that soda that tastes so good and has no calories, or that cell phone that you can get for free with any trade-in—always appealing to our physical and emotional impulses.

Money itself can be an insatiable impulse. Those who embezzle or create Ponzi schemes can never get enough money. The more money they get, the more they want. But money is not the only enticing thing the world offers. Fame is at least equal to it. The more likes someone gets on a social media site, the more they want. Any human passion is susceptible to addiction. And addiction is the number one tool of the adversary.

So we all walk a short tightrope trying to meet our physical and emotional needs—we all need food, clothing, and shelter—but we all know that we can eat too much food, buy too much clothing, and lust after too large a home. That's the central challenge of mortality—overcoming the natural man and woman that would yield to the excesses that the world pushes on us.

When Jesus walked the Earth, he was always trying to help his followers understand who they really were—not who they thought they were or who they thought others thought they were—but who they really were: children of God. In Luke 9:23, we read, "If any man will come after me, let him deny himself, and to take up his cross daily, and follow me."

What does it mean to take up our cross daily? In the JST version of Matthew 16:26, we read: "And now for a man to take up his cross, is to deny himself all ungodliness, and every worldly lust, and keep my commandments."

I like the following thought from a religious leader, Samuel G. Candler:

> To "take up our cross," however, means to lay our strengths aside. It means to lay our "ego strength" aside. Taking up our cross means, instead, picking up those weaknesses that we so often try to run away from in life. Taking up our cross means carrying around those places we are vulnerable, places where we are maybe even exposed to embarrassment and shame.[51]

So Jesus was asking his followers to bring their weaknesses with them, acknowledge them, and then let Him through his grace give them strength to make weak things become strong— as it says in Ether in the Book of Mormon. Reading from the Joseph Smith translation:

> And whosoever will lose his life in this world, for my sake, shall find it in the world to come. Therefore, forsake the world, and save your souls; for what is a man profited, if he shall gain the whole world, and lose his own soul? Or what shall a man give in exchange for his soul? (JST Matthew 16:28–29).

In other words, if we focus on our own ego, our own needs and wants, we will never break away from the natural man or woman, and we will never come to know who we really are. This is the clincher. When we constantly go after our own needs and wants, we get hooked on worldly things. We begin to identify ourselves by the clothes we wear, the house we live in, or the car we drive. Our identity shifts from our spiritual self to material things. Not much compassion here.

The things of the world are tangible, present, and easily obtained. But possessions do not define us—not at all. They can get in our way.

---

51. Samuel G. Candler, *What Does It Mean to 'Take Up Your Cross?'*, 18 March 2012, https://www.cathedralatl.org/sermons/what-does-it-mean-to-take-up-your-cross/.

They can make us think we're making progress when instead we're giving up what really matters. It has been said that we can become possessed by our possessions. Material things can take over our lives. We can spend far too much time maintaining, repairing, renewing, and upgrading everything we buy.

This is what Jesus was trying to teach us. We can lose ourselves to the world. But when we lose ourselves in service to Him and to those around us, we can find our true identity as His children and His followers. Every time we do His will, we are drawn closer to Him and further away from worldly things. And when we're drawn closer to Him, we discover our inherent worth. We discover that we are of infinite worth—that the things with price tags are of little worth, but we are worth everything. We need to imagine ourselves as being of infinite worth because we might even feel worthless at times. This requires compassionate imagination: seeing ourselves as God sees us. Forgiving ourselves for our weaknesses. Letting His love overcome our inadequacies.

When we begin to get a glimpse of our worth and our true identity, we want to take care of ourselves so that we can care for others. We want to do what God wants us to—take up our cross and follow Him. When we take up our cross, we relate to others with the same compassion God has for us. Taking up our cross means that we have compassion for ourselves as well as for others. Only then can we release our imagination so that it can carry our thoughts on eagles' wings and help us see how we can fulfill God's will for us.

While serving as a general officer of the church, I was hosted by General Authority Seventies, who presided over many areas of the worldwide church. These are humble servants who have taken up their cross and followed the Savior. They often find out where they will serve only briefly before they pack their bags and depart. They serve for years in far distant places, sometimes in cultures and languages new to them. I knew one newly called Seventy who learned that he would be assigned to an area presidency and assumed he would serve in a country that spoke Spanish since that was the language he learned on his mission. However, when the assignment came, he was placed in an area presidency in Asia. He took a deep breath and began working on Chinese.

I once accompanied a General Authority Seventy to Albania. As soon as we left the airport, we went directly to the home of two adult sisters who suffered from the same terminal illness. They had not been able to obtain any healthcare to ease their suffering, and they were anxious to receive a blessing from a servant of the Lord. We laid our hands on the first sister and then the second. Their faith was tangible. Following the blessings, we were driving away from the home to our next appointment, but the image of those sweet sisters stayed with me. They knew they would die from their disease, but the blessings gave them the courage to face whatever suffering lay before them. The Seventy's compassion, I believe, helped them imagine a better world to come.

Each of the Seventies I encountered was unique in personality. But they all have one thing that comes through resoundingly. They are committed to serve wherever they are called for however long they are asked to serve there. Some members might imagine their service sounds exciting and exotic—watching over the Church in a foreign country. But I can attest that it is hard work. They lay their ego strength aside. Their service is not about them; it's about building the Kingdom. I was inspired by the dedication of these general authorities and their families for how they took up their cross and followed the Savior. I want to have that same dedication.

CHAPTER 24

OVERCOME DIFFERENCES WITH COMPASSION

A BISHOP ONCE RECOUNTED THE FOLLOWING STORY THAT SHOWS COMpassionate imagination's power. The story shows how unity comes when we overlook differences and see each other as children of God.

> Jeff and his male partner had not been to church in thirty years. His partner had been battling cancer for some time, but the disease finally took him. His dying wish was to have his funeral in our church building. I worked out the arrangements with Jeff. The funeral took place, and it was a beautiful service. During the funeral, I met some of Jeff's family. After the service, I invited Jeff to attend church the next day. He didn't commit but said he'd think about it. I told him that 90% of the congregation would welcome him with open arms and 10% might wonder why he was there. But I told him that he would be overwhelmed by the love he would feel from the 90%.
>
> I thought there had to be some reason his partner requested that his funeral be held in our chapel. He must have had positive feelings toward the Church even though he had not attended for a long time. Sunday came, but he did not enter the church building. I took my place on the stand next to President Smith, a counselor in the stake presidency. I was conducting that day, and even though it was time for the meeting to begin, for some reason, I hesitated. I

still wondered if he might come. Then, I leaned over to ask President Smith if he wanted me to begin the meeting. But as I was asking him, I saw Jeff walk in and begin looking for a seat in the back of the chapel. So, even though it was time to begin the meeting, I knew I should welcome Jeff instead of standing at the podium.

I felt as if I was lifted out of my chair. So I told President Smith to wait a minute. I walked back through the main chapel and the entire gym to the back door to give him a big hug and a warm welcome. I introduced him to two nearby families who gave him big welcome hugs and showed how happy they were to meet him.

One of the members had attended the funeral service the day before. Following the meeting, one of those members invited Jeff to attend Thanksgiving dinner with his family. They have continued to invite him almost every year, and another family in the congregation invited him to spend Christmas with them. He has felt welcome ever since and enjoys attending services whenever he's in town. I still call him periodically and reminisce about those moments that helped him return to activity in the church.

This might seem like a simple act of kindness, but I see it as much more than that. The bishop was not the only one who reached out to Jeff. Others in the ward embraced him and made him feel the Christlike unity that can come only through the gospel of Jesus Christ. Compassionate imagination: the bishop had to imagine that ward members would welcome Jeff, and they did. Jeff had to imagine that the bishop would consider his request to hold the funeral in the chapel, even though he and his deceased partner had never felt comfortable entering the doors.

I envision that if any members were uncomfortable with the funeral or with Jeff coming back to the church, their hearts might have softened when they met him and saw other members reaching out to him with such warmth and acceptance. As Elder Gerrit Gong has helped us understand, we need to make this church a refuge for all.[52] We want all members to imagine the compassion they will feel if they gather the courage to return.

Jeff felt Christlike unity with the other members of the ward because they reached out to him through love. They acted in faith—a faith born of compassion and imagination. This is how Jesus reached out to others

---

52. Gerrit W. Gong, Room in the Inn, General Conference, The Church of Jesus Christ of Latter-day Saints, Apr. 2021, Gospel Library App.

when He was here upon the earth. When He came across people who were different, He did not shy away. He embraced them, and they felt His love. We can all do that for those whose sexual orientation may be different from our own.

CHAPTER 25

STRENGTHEN RELATIONSHIPS AND BUILD CHRISTLIKE UNITY

WE KNOW RELATIONSHIPS ARE ESSENTIAL TO OUR HAPPINESS ON EARTH and throughout eternity. Exaltation will come to those whose relationships are healthy and loving. So why do we avoid focusing on them as much as we might? To strengthen a relationship, we need to act in faith with compassion and imagination.

Matthew 5 has great potential to draw us closer to the Savior. The stories in the New Testament hold our attention. They're beautiful and inspiring, but in Matthew 5, Jesus teaches us how to become more like him in only a few verses. He tells us that he came not to replace the law of Moses—the Ten Commandments—but to fulfill them. What does that mean? He begins by saying:

> Ye have heard that it was said by them of old time, Thou shalt not kill; and whosoever shall kill shall be in danger of the judgment: But I say unto you, That whosoever is angry with his brother without a cause shall be in danger of the judgment (Matthew 5:21–22).

So we might conclude that if someone else makes us mad, it's OK. It's only bad to get angry if no one else provokes us to anger. But wait a minute, a better translation is found in 3 Nephi. And, oops, that excuse seems to have evaporated. In 3 Nephi 12:22, we read, "But I say unto you, that whosoever is angry with his brother shall be in danger of his judgment." The phrase "without a cause" disappeared. My interpretation is that we should avoid anger—at least the kind that leads to lashing out at someone else. Jesus's message is that words can kill our spirit, just as a bullet can kill our body. You've likely heard the saying, "Sticks and stones can break my bones, but words will never hurt me." The fact is that words can not only hurt us; they can kill us.

Recently, 20-year old Michelle Carter [was] found guilty of involuntary manslaughter and sentenced to two and a half years in prison. This is an unprecedented case in that Carter sent texts to her friend, Conrad Roy III, telling him to kill himself. Roy, who was 18, rigged a generator to his pickup truck, jumped in the vehicle and died of carbon monoxide poisoning.

Words actually killed that young man. So we turn that old saying around: Sticks and stones can break my bones, but words can kill you."[53]

You might wonder why the scriptures say that God gets angry—that sometimes his anger is kindled against us. I do not believe that the phrase means God lashes out in rage. It means that He is frustrated that we do not understand the meaning of Christ's Atonement and the power of His mercy and grace.

In his book *Bonds That Make Us Free*, my good friend Terry Warner says that the source of relational anger is "self-betrayal" (p.40).[54] He argues that people sometimes turn to anger in the selfish justification of thoughts or behaviors. In such cases, individuals act in ways that betray personal values, and instead of correcting their mistaken perspectives, these individuals feel anger and blame it on another person or object. Anger and blame then create contention that can plant the seed for ongoing relational conflict.

Let's bring this close to home—our home. Recently, our furnace stopped working. The temperature outside dropped into the single digits, and our inside temperature kept falling. I looked online and called a heating and air-conditioning company with "emergency service." I liked

---

53. "Words Can Kill . . . and Do," *C-Suite Network* https://c-suitenetwork.com/articles/words-can-kill-and-do/.
54. C. Terry Warner, B*onds That Make Us Free: Healing Our Relationships, Coming to Ourselves* (Salt Lake City: Deseret Book Company, 2016), p.40.

the term *emergency* because, at 4 a.m., our house was getting colder and colder. When I got the answering service, the receptionist said, "Yes, we could have someone to your home between 8 a.m. and noon." I said, "Don't get me wrong, I'm not complaining, but what does "emergency" mean? She said, "You'll need to ask the service rep when he gets to your home. I can't answer that question."

I wasn't angry, but I was a little frustrated. I could've lashed out at her and said, "Wait just a minute; I thought you gave emergency service!" I could have hung up on her in anger. There were lots of ways to show my anger, but I would have been betraying myself, as Terry Warner said. I would've been going against my beliefs and values. When the Lord said, "Love one another," He didn't say "unless they let you down or unless they fail to do what you want them to do." He said, "Love one another." That means everyone.

Later in Matthew 5, Jesus says that we should even love those who wrong us: "You have heard that it hath been said, Thou shalt love thy neighbour, and hate thine enemy. But I say unto you, Love your enemies, bless them that curse you, do good to them that hate you" (verses 43–44).

This is an amazing passage! Love our enemies? Even those who disagree with us? Even those who try to cheat us out of our money? Think of the effect this one bit of counsel would have on the world—no more war. The Book of Mormon teaches us very clearly that enemies can be turned into friends. The Lamanites, who joined the church after Ammon and his brothers taught them the gospel, began to love those they once hated. They did not betray themselves. They lived up to the highest in them. They did not let their dark side overcome the light of Christ that was within.

So what should we do when we get frustrated or upset with someone or know someone is upset with us? Matthew 5 provides the answer. "Therefore if thou bring thy gift to the altar, and there rememberest that thy brother hath ought against thee; leave there thy gift before the altar, and go thy way; first be reconciled to thy brother, and then come and offer thy gift (versus 23–24).

This is powerful. In today's language, if I go to the temple and then I remember that someone feels that I have wronged them, I should leave the temple and go see the one I know has ill feelings against me. Of course, the reverse is true also. If I have bad feelings towards someone else, I should go resolve the dispute before going to the temple.

When we were serving as temple president and matron, I was standing in the hallway ready to close the door before a session was to begin, and a brother exited the endowment room and motioned for me to close the door, leaving him in the hallway with me. I thought he might have a health problem, but he turned to me and said, "I can't be in the same session as that brother on the back row." In other words, he said he had ought with his brother and couldn't resolve the dispute inside the endowment room, so he would wait for the next session. Of course, the ideal solution would have been for both of them to exit and meet in a private room to resolve their differences.

Lolly: I had an experience in the temple that taught me much about judging others. I had no compassionate imagination in this instance. We were waiting in the chapel for the session to move to the instruction room. A gentleman I had seen before in the temple was speaking rather loudly to the coordinator at the rear of the chapel. They eventually stepped outside the room, but their voices seemed just as loud. I was having trouble concentrating and asked Russ if he was bothered. "No," he said, "I just block it out." I couldn't block it out and became frustrated at the intrusion. Because I was with my sister, we took the elevator with the one who had been talking loudly, and the conversation continued just as loudly. Then, in the endowment room, this brother kept chatting and moving about as we waited for the others.

As the session began, I was suddenly reminded that Russ most likely would want to participate in the prayer circle, and I still had unkind thoughts toward this brother. I knew I needed to repent. The session was small, and even if I didn't go to the prayer circle, this brother would be in the circle. I turned my thoughts to the Savior and thought about how He must see this brother. I prayed and prayed and finally received awareness of God's love for him and me. I felt a change of heart; a feeling of oneness and love came over me.

We almost ran into the brother as I entered the Celestial room with my sister. Using a temple voice this time, he told us, "How nice you are here as sisters!" We agreed, and I asked him if he went to the temple with his brother. "No," he said, "he can't come anymore, so I come alone." This faithful brother was alone and came to the Lord's house to feel connection. I had never seen him with a spouse. He was perhaps hard of hearing, a possible reason for his loud voice. He had difficulty standing and moved toward the curtain, where he could lean against the folding door during the prayer circle. Whatever his infirmities, he was doing the very best he could. Hopefully, I will not need to relearn this lesson repeatedly.

What happened to Lolly happens to most of us at some point. Someone's behavior upsets us. And when anger enters a relationship or when there is an unresolved dispute, there is self-betrayal going on. We are not rising to a higher, holier way. We're not showing love to everyone. We are allowing our dark side to rule. But when love rules, when reconciliation occurs, when tempers subside, we draw closer to God and to each other, as Lolly felt closer to the brother whose behavior had earlier been bothersome. She let the dark side go and turned to the Light.

When anger builds up, slow down, reconsider, breathe deeply, and then talk your frustration through in prayer in a reasoned, calm way. Envision the others as God sees them. The frustration served its purpose. It brought you to a resolution. And we all need more of that in our lives. Compassionate imagination leads us away from anger. We imagine our way out of anger and toward love. We look upon the person we allowed to make us angry and find compassion for them.

Oh, and how did the furnace turn out? The repair man thought he had it all fixed, fired up the furnace, and no heat came out of the registers. He was ready to give us a bill and take off, but then he had to recheck it. The motor had given out, so it needed to be replaced. So what we thought might be a $100 charge turned into a much larger bill, and we needed to wait a week for the part. But we had to go to California the next day, so we let the house stay cool for a week. That's emergency service. That's mortality.

CHAPTER 26

EXPERIENCE RECONCILIATION

ESTRANGEMENT IS THE OPPOSITE OF CHRISTLIKE UNITY IN RELATION-ships. Nearly one in four adults in the US is estranged from at least one family member.[55] Siblings can become estranged from one another; parents can become estranged from their children. Siblings can be close to one another but unwilling to talk to their parents. It's all about relationships, which is, in one sense, the dark side of relationships. If we want light and love in our relationships, we need to imagine that light and love and then act in faith with compassion toward one another. When one acts in faith with compassionate imagination, estrangement can be replaced by love.

John 1:11 says that we can even become estranged from God. Let's think about that for a moment. How do people distance themselves from God? Some say it happens when we sin, and that's true, but it's probably much more than that. Certainly, when we intentionally hurt someone else with our words or actions, we distance ourselves from God. But even laziness can cause us to forget God. Being so discouraged that we fail to pray can also bring estrangement from God.

When we berate ourselves and forget that we are the spirit children of Heavenly Father, we draw away from God. Recently, I talked with

55. Karl Pillemer, *Fault Lines: Fractured Families and How to Mend Them* (New York City: Avery, 2020), p.4.

someone about Nephi's negative internal chatter. And a lot of that chapter came because he forgot the blessings that God had already given him. Only when he began to remember all of the blessings he had received was the soul awakened so that he could feel close to God again.

Estrangement can be overcome through reconciliation. Nephi reconciled himself to God. And that reconciliation is possible only through Christ's Atonement. Elder Bruce R. McConkie explained it this way:

> Reconciliation is the process of ransoming man from sin and spiritual darkness and restoring him to a state of harmony and unity with Deity.[56]

We don't want to become estranged from a family member, and we do not want to become estranged from God. I believe that when family members draw away from one another, they often draw away from God. They become estranged from both family and God, and the only way back—the only path to reconciliation—is to draw upon the power of Christ's Atonement. Christ came to earth to help us become reconciled to each other and to God. This is how we become alive in Christ. We take His name upon us. We make covenants never to be estranged, and then we keep that covenant. Day in and day out we draw closer to the Savior and closer to our Father in Heaven.

Reconciliation with God or a family member or friend demands that we imagine harmony replacing discord. This may require more imagination than at any other time in our life. One of my Chinese graduate students once said, "I wish I could believe in God, but I grew up being taught there was no God, so I just don't seem to be able to shake that belief." Non-belief had been her "religion" all her life, and replacing that with belief did not seem possible. She needed to free herself from that non-belief and embrace a new way of seeing herself and her relationship with God. She needed to become reconciled to God.

When we sin, we need reconciliation. When we fall short of our own expectations, we need reconciliation. I've always loved the words, "Old things are done away, and all things have become new" (3 Nephi 12:47). Jesus taught that the old law had been fulfilled in Him. Jesus brought newness to the world, a rebirth. He taught us to put old things behind

---

56. Terence M. Vinson, *Reconciled to God*, Gospel Essays, October 2014, https://www.churchofjesuschrist.org/study/ensign/2014/10/reconciled-to-god?lang=eng.

us and look forward to a brighter, more joyful future. Elder McConkie taught that reconciliation can help us become new creatures in Christ. My hope is to let old things pass away and all become new. Let old beliefs go and let imagination fill our minds with how things might be. Let estrangement be replaced by reconciliation.

CHAPTER 27

REMEMBER THE
MAGIC WORD: YET

LOLLY: WE WERE PRIVILEGED TO SERVE AS VIRTUAL BYU-PATHWAY MIS-sionaries for two years. Our son, who was living in the Caribbean, asked us if we might be interested in helping establish BYU-Pathway on some English-speaking islands where he served as a counselor in the district presidency. District leaders, with approval of mission leaders, requested that we train young full-time missionaries serving on these islands after COVID to help recruit potential students—both members and friends of the church.

The first semester course covered a lot: time management, financial planning, goal setting—all kinds of topics. At the end of each semester, we asked our students to reflect on their experience and share their favorite lesson with the group in our weekly online gathering. A 50-year-old woman who began her studies thinking that she would never be able to succeed in a college course responded without prodding:

> Oh, that's easy for me. The most important thing I learned was about the fixed and growth mindsets. I had never heard of that idea before, and it changed everything. And now, here I am at the end of the semester, and I've succeeded, even though I knew I would fail. Yes, fixed and growth mindsets—that changed my life.

You've probably heard of this concept. It's been around a long time. Carol Dweck, a Stanford psychologist, developed the theory. It's simple: someone with a fixed mindset places limits on themselves, and someone with a growth mindset believes that their potential is far greater than their current performance.

Carol Dweck happens to be my age, so she grew up in psychology during my era. In those early days, IQ was everything. Psychologists have always been enamored with measuring human characteristics, so they thought we needed to learn how to measure intelligence. But psychologists were never satisfied with simply getting a number. They wanted that number to predict future performance. Predictability was the game, so IQ was the ticket. If we want to know how well someone will perform on this task or on that job, let's give them an IQ test, and then we can decide whether to hire the person.

Think of college admissions. If we can figure out how well someone will do in college, we can decide which students to admit and which to reject. So along came entrance exams like the ACT and SAT. Now look at what's happening. Colleges are increasingly reluctant to place too much weight on these exams for admissions. Some universities are eliminating them entirely. Why? The tests are often less predictive than one might have hoped. And most importantly, they are culturally biased.

IQ tests were notoriously culturally biased. I remember administering an IQ test to a young boy who had grown up in Hawaii. Question: "Snow is to white as grass is to_____." The boy said, "rain." Of course, the correct answer is "green". But if you've never seen snow before, the question is problematic. It's culturally biased.

Alfred Binet, a French psychologist, invented the IQ test. Why did he create it? To help French educators identify those with severe disabilities who needed special educational help. But then, when IQ tests came to this country, we wanted to use them for all sorts of things. Over a century ago, a Stanford psychologist, Lewis Terman, turned the IQ test into a pervasive instrument, taking it far beyond its original purpose.[57] So it's only appropriate that a referendum on the IQ test came from a more

---

57. European Medical, "Binet compared to Terman," Cognitive Therapy (2023), https://www.europeanmedical.info/cognitive-therapy/binet-compared-to-terman.html.

recent Stanford psychologist, Carol Dweck. Dweck's research showed that people can change, that IQ may be a static number, but it does not predict one's potential. She argued in favor of a "growth mindset" rather than a "fixed mindset:"

> The fixed mindset limits achievement. It fills people's minds with interfering thoughts, it makes effort disagreeable, and it leads to inferior learning strategies. What's more, it makes other people into judges instead of allies..[58]

Lolly: When I was teaching sixth-grade math, we administered a battery of tests at the beginning of the year in order to group our students. As teachers, we ranked the students according to their scores and arbitrarily divided them into three equal groups. I taught the highest group, and every year, three or four students would come to me and ask if there was any way they could be included in the high math group. After talking with their parents and assessing each student's desires— even though we had limited desks and books, I always said, "How about we give you a two-week trial? If, after the first test, you still want to be in the class, we'll somehow find room for you."

I found that these students often outperformed the students who had much higher scores on the tests taken at the beginning. They worked harder, sought help more often, and did their homework diligently. After experiencing success, they felt more confident and received high marks throughout the year. A few years after I retired, I saw the mother of one of these borderline students going out of the temple. She thanked me for teaching her daughter and then told me that she had received the top award in geometry in middle school and was thinking of becoming a math major.

From a gospel perspective, we know that when we act in faith, we can accomplish more than we ever thought possible. The greater our faith, the more faithful action we can take, and the greater our chance for success. When we understand our God-given potential, no test should hold

---

58. Carol S. Dweck, *Mindset: The New Psychology of Success*, (New York City: Ballantine Books, 2007), p.66.

us back. A test is a temporary measure, not a predictor of our potential. When we imagine achieving a particular goal—a goal that God wants us to achieve—his grace will help us accomplish it. This is a result of compassionate imagination.

Dweck's critique of the IQ test for me was right on. President Hinckley said something similar about the relationship between work and talents: "Work is the miracle by which talent is brought to the surface and dreams become reality."[59] It's all about acting in faith. In other words, the gifts and talents we are given are much less important than the effort we spend developing them. More recently, President Nelson said: "Resolve to be resolute. The Lord loves effort."[60]

Our 50-year-old Pathway student did not see herself as intellectually gifted. Still, she became resolute and exerted real effort, and so she succeeded in a college course—all because of work and her exercise of faith. As a grandmother, she outperformed her expectations, just as Lolly's sixth-grade students did. They acted in faith. They exemplified what Dweck and Presidents Hinckley and Nelson declared. No test knows our potential. Only God knows our potential, and He has made it clear what that potential is—to become like Him.

How does all this apply to finding Christlike unity in relationships? Those with a fixed mindset place limits on themselves and their relationships. They might say, "Well, I'm not very enjoyable to be around; I'm not very good at conversation." Or "I'm not good at meeting people; I'm no good with names; I can't remember faces." And the list goes on and on. Very little self-compassion and severely limited imagination. They have difficulty envisioning themselves forming healthy relationships and feeling a sense of belonging or unity.

Those with a growth mindset might say, "You know, I'm not very good with names yet, or I'm not very good in conversations yet." Notice that word: *yet*. This is the hallmark of the growth mindset. Instead of saying, "I'm not good at math," you say, "I'm not good at math yet, but I could be if I act in faith." The word *yet* is an imagination word. You

---

59. Gordon B. Hinckley, *To a Man Who Has Done What This Church Expects of Each of Us*, BYU Speeches, 17 October 1995, https://speeches.byu.edu/talks/gordon-b-hinckley/man-done-church-expects-us/.

60. Russell M. Nelson, "President Russell M. Nelson suggests 3 resolutions in his first message of 2022," *Church News,* January 1, 2022, https://www.thechurchnews.com/2022/1/1/23265689/president-russell-m-nelson-suggests-3-resolutions-in-his-first-message-of-2022.

envision the future and imagine your success. In other words, your current level of performance has almost nothing to do with your ultimate potential. Your ultimate potential depends on how much effort you want to expend and how much faith you want to exert.

In relationships, the concept goes even further. I can impose a fixed mindset on someone else without even recognizing it. I can say, "I don't think that person likes me." But maybe that person could like you with the right experiences, effort, and faith. You need to use your imagination and have compassion for yourself and for the other person. Compassion means giving yourself and others space; you don't limit yourself or others.

Relationships are constantly evolving. So we need to let them evolve and grow. With a growth mindset, we nurture growth in each other. We help others reach their potential. We have compassion for each other. One of our primary goals is to help our friend or spouse achieve all they were meant to achieve in this life. That potential will not be reached if either person has a fixed mindset.

I am sure you see how this applies in a gospel sense. The Lord does not want us to place limits on ourselves. Rather, He wants us to strive for perfection even if that divine state will not happen until the next life. "Perfection is pending," as President Nelson has said.[61] The Lord wants us to become like Him. And that means growing in holiness every day. And the only way that can happen is if we draw closer to Him—if we strive to become one with Him. As we strive to become one with the Lord, we will experience unity with others. We will imagine our way to Christlike unity as we compassionately relate to one another.

How do we know when we fall prey to a fixed mindset? In my view, it's when we allow negative internal chatter to take over. Negative internal chatter places limits on us and prevents us from reaching our potential. We might say, "There's no use in trying to improve this marriage. It is what it is." Or, "I'm not going to try and make amends to my sister; I know she'll just reject me, so I'll just leave things as they are." Fixed mindset. Negative internal chatter. When these things take over, we need to take a step back and reassess. We need to exchange that fixed mindset for a growth mindset: "Things aren't like I want them to be yet." Add that one word, and you will be more likely to try again. And with the Lord's help, success will come. Let the word *yet* cause you to fire

---

61. Russell M. Nelson, Perfection Pending, *Ensign*, General Conference, The Church of Jesus Christ of Latter-day Saints, Oct. 1995, Gospel Library App.

up your imagination. Begin to see yourself in new ways. Have compassion on yourself for past mistakes or shortcomings. To become more like God, envision yourself with the qualities you seek.

This word *yet* can help parents. When a child says, "She doesn't like me!" You could say, "You mean she doesn't like you yet." When a child says, "I'm not good at math or English or science," you can say, "You mean you're not good yet." This can lead to another conversation about desire. "Do you want to be good? I can help you become good if you want to." I wish everyone could use the word *yet* more often to help one another move to a growth mindset so that we can imagine ourselves the way we wish we could be. This is what the Lord wants us to do—to open ourselves to our true potential and avoid closing ourselves off to what could be the most fulfilling, joy-filled experiences of our lives. Remember the word *yet*!

CHAPTER 28

RELY ON COVENANTS AND CONSISTENCY

When I was growing up, like most other children, I thought all parents were like mine, but as I spent time with my friends' families, I began to see many differences. My mother, for example, was more committed to cleanliness in our home than were some of my friends' mothers. She wanted the windows washed almost weekly, the tops of the door frames dusted regularly, and the kitchen floor mopped and waxed every Saturday. Sometimes, after vacuuming the living room, I'd say, "Mom, I am done, but I can't tell the difference." She would reply, "That's OK, because I can tell the difference."

My mom was committed to cleanliness, and both of my parents were committed to the Lord. Dad always woke me up an hour before priesthood meeting so we could arrive a half hour before the meeting began and help prepare for the meeting. We almost always beat the bishopric to the church. My Dad held no position that would cause him to do that. He was just committed. I never questioned my parents' testimonies of the Restoration, even though I cannot remember either bearing their testimony. The way they lived their lives was their witness to the Lord that they loved him. Reflecting on it now, I don't think they knew any other way to act in faith.

I've often wondered how best to describe my parents. They were seldom in the spotlight. Consistency has to be at the top of all their qualities I admire. Consistency is not usually lauded as the loftiest human quality. But the consistency of my parents, I'm convinced, had a powerful positive effect on my life. I could always count on them. They never shocked me with a sudden change of mind. They knew who they were and what they valued in life and spent their days pursuing those values. Family therapy research has shown that when parents are consistent, their children reap a boatload of blessings.[62] The child can count on the parent to react in certain ways, to be there in times of need, and to show constant love. No flip-flopping. No unpredictability. Just consistent parental love.

One psychologist, although he didn't realize it, described the kind of consistency I recognized in my parents:

> Being consistent is not the same as being boring. It is not the same as being totally predictable, either. People who are consistent can be fun, creative, innovative, adventure-seeking, expansive, even spontaneous in many different ways.
>
> The difference is that they are predictable in certain core ways. They are predictable in whom and what they prioritize. They are predictable in making decisions based on a clear set of internal values and not the immediate circumstances. They have consistent moral compasses that aren't affected by who or what is around them at the time. They are predictable in the big things that they want. They are predictable in that when you go to them with a problem or issue, you know what you are going to get. They stick to their principles regardless of the weather. Consistent people are the ones who become trusted leaders, loyal friends, and life-long partners. They are the folks on whom you can depend when the going gets tough, which happens often in life.[63]

My parents were examples of this kind of consistency. I knew I could always count on them. Without knowing anything about relationship

---

62. Stephanie Cox, "Why Consistent Parenting Is So Important, and So Hard," *Psychology Today* (2022), https://www.psychologytoday.com/us/blog/family-prep/202202/why-consistent-parenting-is-so-important-and-so-hard#:~:text=Consistency%20is%20the%20most%20effective,learning,%20just%20as%20you%20are.

63. Bruce Y. Lee, "The One Consistent Thing to Look for in a Person," *Psychology Today*, 15 February 2023, https://www.psychologytoday.com/us/blog/a-funny-bone-to-pick/202302/the-one-consistent-thing-to-look-for-in-a-person.

theories, my parents made exploring my world, experimenting, and seeking new knowledge comfortable, even enticing. Long before Wikipedia, we had the World Book in our home and The Book of Knowledge—an encyclopedia aimed at young people. Not only did we have these resources in our home, but we used them to answer questions that would pop up. And my parents always provided a feeling of safety. As children, my siblings and I knew we could trust them to do what they said they would do. It was often easy to act in faith because we observed them acting in faith. They helped us develop a growth mindset and allowed us to imagine how to improve and find success.

Crime would drop dramatically if children grew up in this kind of world. Emotional illness would occur much less frequently and be less severe. Prejudice and discrimination would largely evaporate if all parents could consistently keep their covenants. Children need consistency because consistency allows trust to grow, and when trust grows, all kinds of human misery will end.

Speaking of the importance of consistency, Elder L. Todd Budge described how his son became very ill on his mission in Africa:

> Our son . . . was taken to a medical facility with limited resources. As we read his first letter to us after his illness, we expected that he would be discouraged, but instead he wrote,
>
> "Even as I lay in the emergency room, I felt peace. I have never been so consistently and resiliently happy in my life." As my wife and I read these words, we were overcome with emotion. *Consistently and resiliently happy.* We had never heard happiness described that way, but his words rang true. We knew that the happiness he described was not simply pleasure or an elevated mood but a peace and joy that come when we surrender ourselves to God and trust Him in *all things*.[64]

I believe Elder Budge's son felt consistently and resiliently happy due to the covenants he had made with God. He knew he could trust God. He knew that God would never break his promises. Their son knew that no matter what happened to him physically, he would be fine spiritually—all because of covenants. I also believe that the Budges provided the same example of acting in faith that my parents provided because of

---

64. L. Todd Budge, *Consistent and Resilient Trust*, General Conference, The Church of Jesus Christ of Latter-day Saints, Oct. 2019, Gospel Library App.

the covenants they had made with each other and with God. They provided a home filled with consistency, as did my parents. Their son was born in the covenant. He was enveloped in the power of the covenant. He knew that. And so he was "consistently and resiliently happy" and at peace no matter what lay ahead.

Our love for the Lord increases when we keep our covenants and act in faith. When we keep our covenants, our trust in the Lord increases. Covenants are binding, strengthening, and sure. Elder Budge's son felt love, trust, and the strengthening power that comes—and can only come—from making sacred covenants with God. As parents, we are not perfectly consistent, but God is perfectly consistent, and the more we keep our covenants, the more we feel that consistency. When we keep covenants, we grow closer to God and approach oneness with him. Covenant keeping also leads to unity in our family and with others. When we make covenants, we feel the Lord's compassion for us, and when we keep covenants, we share that compassion with others.

CHAPTER 29

BELIEVE THAT WITH GOD, NOTHING IS IMPOSSIBLE

IN THE BOOK OF JOHN, JESUS COMPARES HIMSELF TO THE VINE AND HIS disciples to the branches attached to the vine. When we abide in Christ, we can achieve all that he wants us to do:

> Abide in me, and I in you. As the branch cannot bear fruit of itself, except it abide in the vine; no more can ye, except ye abide in me. I am the vine, ye are the branches: He that abideth in me, and I in him, the same bringeth forth much fruit: for without me ye can do nothing (John 15:4–5).

Through the power of Christ's Atonement, we can fulfill our purpose here on the earth. And without His power, we can do nothing. This passage reminds me of the verse, "With God nothing shall be impossible" (Luke 1:37). I had an experience a long time ago that showed me that even when someone has a disability, they can succeed if they abide in Christ and embrace compassionate imagination. Here's a brief version of that experience.

It was early in the spring. I was seated at my desk in the graduate student room, and my advisor—the professor who chaired my doctoral committee—approached me and asked if I would be willing to tutor a 14-year-old boy in reading. He explained that the boy's mother was willing to pay me if I could tutor her son three times per week. I remember feeling conflicted because I needed the money, but I did not feel that I was skilled enough to help a young man who had failed for so long to learn how to read.

When I met this boy (I'll call him Nick), I was surprised, not only by his appearance—he was taller than I had imagined—but also by his manner. A friendly, easy-to-talk-to kid with a warm smile, Nick looked like the all-American boy, not someone who had been worn down by years of what I assumed had been a continual failure in the classroom.

I first wanted to get a feel for his general intellectual ability, and since I had just completed a master's degree in school psychology and knew how to administer the WISC IQ test, I asked Nick to take a seat while I gave the test to him. His IQ, as measured by this test, was 122, which meant he was mildly gifted. Following that test, I administered a reading exam. During this exam, I asked Nick to name the letters of the alphabet, produce the phonetic sounds of each letter, and read simple sight words, such as *the* and *there*.

Nick's IQ score predicted that he should be reading well above grade level, but the reading test showed he was reading on a pre-primer level. In other words, this gifted 14-year-old young man was reading at the same level as a four- to five-year-old. I must admit that I was more than surprised. I had a hard time understanding how Nick could be so bright and not be able to distinguish a *d* from a *b* or an *m* from an *n*. Neither was he able to read the simple sight words, such as *is* or *this*. It was baffling to me and a little daunting—especially with my inexperience teaching reading. I had to imagine that he could succeed, and he had to imagine it as well. In the parlance of the growth mindset, he could not read—*yet*.

Then, when I spoke with Nick's mother, my concerns grew even worse. She explained how she had done everything she could to help Nick learn to read. She had enrolled him in several expensive private programs—all to no avail. His reading ability didn't budge. He seemed permanently stuck at the pre-primer level. He was in the ninth grade—so all those years of schooling had done almost nothing to help him learn how to read. She also described how her husband had the same disability. He was a builder but had to ask someone else to read the blueprints because he could not read at all.

Even though I was hesitant in some ways because I didn't want to be a part of another failure experience for Nick, I was also determined to see if I could help him. He wanted to learn, so I wanted to help him. We used a manual entitled *Beginning Reading 1* by Grant Von Harrison, my graduate advisor. We began our tutoring sessions by learning a few letter sounds, then how to blend those sounds into words, adding sight words (words that are not phonetic). Nick was doing quite well. He gradually became more proficient at blending sounds into words. The challenge was learning the sight words. If he saw the word *it*, he was just as likely to say *that*. Even though the words do not look anything alike, he could not keep them straight. He might say the word correctly five times in a row and then miss it the next five times. He had classic dyslexia.

So we kept working and helping him with sight words, but the phonetic skills had much more impact on his reading ability than the practice with sight words. After several months, I asked if he would like to try reading a regular book because, up to that time, we had been reading guided exercises. He wanted to try. He said, "I've never even tried to read a whole book before!" So we began with *The Boxcar Children*. This book is on about the fourth grade reading level. It took us weeks, but the satisfaction on Nick's face was worth every minute of the instruction. Once he knew he could read that whole book, he wanted to read more. His mother was ecstatic, and I was ecstatic. His reading level had increased five years' worth in about nine months.

After graduating from high school, Nick served a mission where he learned sign language. He later became certified as a sign language interpreter, which led to a career working with those with hearing impairments.

What lessons do I take from the experience I had with Nick? I learned these important things:

1. Nick had divine help as he learned how to read. I witnessed firsthand how he drew close to the Lord and became determined to beat his dyslexia. I'll never know why he had to wait for this help until he was 14, but I believe the help was real. He learned some complex phonetic skills and one day, he asked, "Are there any more rules like this?" I told him he had learned all the rules he needed to sound out almost any word he would ever encounter.

2. When we have problems as severe as Nick's, one-on-one help may be the only answer—especially when both learner and tutor pray for divine help. I remember sitting with Nick on the grass on a summer day as he read from *The Boxcar Children*, and I helped him with words he had trouble with. I could almost see his motivation increase with even the smallest progress. He could sense he was improving, even though the improvement was slow. But he knew he was getting better at reading, which made him want to work harder every day. Nick's problem was dyslexia, but we all have problems we wish we could overcome.

3. Relationships matter. Nick and I grew to be friends. I was not quite old enough to be his father, but he probably looked at me much like someone would look at a parent. He knew that I had confidence in him. He knew that I would never laugh at a mistake he made. He knew that I would help him only if he needed help, but I was always there to give him just enough guidance and praise to eventually make it on his own. We all need this kind of relationship in our life. As a good friend once said, "Everybody needs a missionary. And what is a missionary? Someone who helps another person do what first seems impossible." So I was like a missionary to Nick, and he could sense it.

4. We should never write someone off. In other words, we never give up on another person. I never met Nick's dad, but I believe many people wrote him off as he grew up. His dyslexia was so severe that they gave up trying to help him. Do I believe that Nick's father could have learned to read? Absolutely. Do I believe his dyslexia was so severe that he was beyond help? Definitely not. But he did not get the right help at the right time. We need to look at ourselves and ask if we are getting the right kind of help with our problems at the right time. We also need to look at others and ask if they're getting the right kind of help at the right time. This is why acting in faith is a key feature of compassionate imagination.

5. Learning is what life is all about. Those who live the fullest lives keep learning every day. Learning changes us, and it can

change those we are close to. Those nine months with Nick helped make it possible for him to reach out to others and help them. What a huge payoff in a relatively short time. When one asks in faith—and both Nick and I had to have faith that he could succeed—there's always a residual spinoff effect. Compassionate imagination always leads to more acts of faith. Nick's success eventually led to the success of the students with hearing impairment he helped as an interpreter. This is the power of compassionate imagination.

The Lord is interested in our success. He went from grace to grace. He learned as He matured. His learning did not come instantly or without effort. He progressed precept upon precept. So it is with us. If you have some ability you would like to increase, I hope you will remember Nick, act in faith, and imagine future success. If Nick could learn to read, we can learn to do anything we need to learn to fulfill our purpose here on earth. As the scriptures say, with God, nothing is impossible.

CHAPTER 30

TAKE JOY IN FREUDENFREUDE

AMMON AND THE SONS OF MOSIAH HAD TO HAVE SUCH IMPRESSIVE imaginations to preach the gospel to people who wanted to kill them. Consider how much faith they had to go among enemies. Christ had not yet come to earth and asked his followers to love their enemies, but Ammon and the Sons of Mosiah knew the principle and practiced it in an amazing way. They eventually saw the Lamanites' hate turn into love. I believe no greater miracle has ever been recorded in scripture than the transformation they witnessed in those they taught. Compassionate imagination? Oh, yes! Even compassion on those who spit upon them, imprisoned them, ran them out of town. Acting in faith? Absolutely! The enmity and deep-rooted hostility of those they came to love could not dissuade them. What far-reaching lessons can we learn from their example?

In the book of Alma, we read that Ammon and his companions did not only take joy in their own success, but they also took joy in the success of their brethren. This is a special emotion—taking joy in others' successes. It's a kind of "let's-rejoice-together" kind of emotion. It's multiplicative. Joy compounds upon joy, as love begets love. Here's the account in Alma: 29:13–15:

Yea, and that same God did establish his church among them; yea, and that same God hath called me by a holy calling, to preach the word unto this people, and hath given me much success, in the which my joy is full. But I do not joy in my own success alone, but my joy is more full because of the success of my brethren, who have been up to the land of Nephi. Behold, they have labored exceedingly, and have brought forth much fruit; and how great shall be their reward!

There is a German word that connotes 'the opposite of' this kind of joy. It's a compound word. The German language is famous for using compound words. One of those words is *schadenfreude*. *Schaden* means harm or damage, and *freude* means joy. So in one compound word, it means taking joy in someone else's misfortune—like when you are happy that a political candidate lost the election because you voted for the opponent. This is not an emotion we seek to develop, but we must admit it exists.

Schadenfreude is not my goal when we think of regulating our own emotions, or definitely not when we think of compassionate imagination. We try not to take joy in someone else's misfortune, even when we see the police pull a reckless driver over and issue a ticket. But there is another German expression, and Germans don't use this word often. But I like it anyway. It makes a lot of sense, especially when we think about acting in faith as one of the essential parts of compassionate imagination. It's the complete opposite of *schadenfreude*. The compound word is *freudenfreude*—taking joy in another's success, just as Ammon and his brethren did so long ago.

Elder Jeffrey R. Holland is a prime example of *freudenfreude*. When a general authority or general officer of the Church speaks in general conference, he doesn't just smile and say, "Good job!" He grabs the speaker's hand and makes him or her feel like the most capable person on the planet. He knows what it means to rejoice together. "That's the best talk on that topic I've ever heard in my life!" he might say. The one receiving his praise knows it's not the best talk, but he makes you feel like it is. There's a feeling of compassion when two people rejoice together in subtle or more obvious ways. Compassion is present when people feel joy. Praise brings with it love. Love brings rejoicing. Rejoicing brings compassion. Maybe it's because when we express *freudenfreude*, we feel

God close, and when we feel God's closeness, we feel His compassion for us—His infinite love.

In the world at present, we see *schadenfreude* almost every day. Fans at sporting events can take joy in the opponent's failure. Sometimes, they get carried away, and their taunts become so vile and repulsive that university administrators need to apologize for their students' behavior. This is *schadenfreude*, and it takes no imagination, and it certainly takes no faith. It's one reason the world is fractured and disunity reigns in so many places.

Freudenfreude is something we should nurture among us. *Freudenfreude* spawns acts of faith. Rejoicing builds up and makes us feel more capable and more able to seek after the goals God wants us to seek. Ammon and his brothers rejoiced in the goodness of God, and the more they rejoiced, the more they found success in extremely difficult circumstances. They had to imagine that success. Then, they had compassion on one another and compassion on themselves when they fell short. As that compassion compounded, they gradually found it easier to act in faith, to draw upon the powers of heaven that are always available, until they had accomplished what God wanted them to do. We can all follow their pattern. We can imagine success. We can rejoice in others' successes. We can draw upon the powers of heaven and act in faith that those powers will keep coming. We can have compassion for others and ourselves in times of trial and challenge. We can rejoice together and find Christlike unity.

CHAPTER 31

FORGIVE THE

UNFORGIVABLE

NOW THAT WE'VE DISCUSSED *FREUDENFREUDE*—THE ACT OF REJOICING together—we can explore how *freudenfreude* relates to one of the most important acts of faith: forgiveness. To illustrate this relationship, I'll share a story from an article in *The Atlantic* by Elizabeth Bruenig.[65]

The story is about James Barber, who killed the grandmother of a woman named Sarah Gregory in 2001. When he killed Sarah's grandmother, he was high on drugs and alcohol, so he did not remember anything about the grisly event. James was no stranger to the family. His girlfriend was Sarah's aunt, so he visited the grandmother's home regularly to see his girlfriend. During that fateful night, when James was stoned, he hit Sarah's grandmother so hard that she died. Sarah could not forgive James. Sarah's anger and hate toward James seemed to increase every year following the murder. Twenty years passed.

As Sarah's anger increased, she noticed that she had difficulty remembering the good qualities of her grandmother; her anger seemed to blot out those memories. Then one day in 2020, Sarah heard a newly released song on the radio by Bruce Springsteen, "Letter to You." She could not get the lyrics out of her mind:

---

65. Elizabeth Breunig, "What It Means to Forgive the Unforgivable," *The Atlantic*, May 2023, https://www.theatlantic.com/ideas/archive/2023/05/james-barber-alabama-death-row-forgiveness/674181/.

I took all my fears and doubts
In my letter to you
All the hard things I found out
In my letter to you.
All that I've found true
And I sent it in my letter to you.[66]

The words of that song caused Sarah to write a letter to James. The following are excerpts from that letter:

Before May 2001, you were part of our family. You saw firsthand how close we were and how we were held together by one woman . . . She was strong, graceful, filled with compassion and love, she forgave and saw the best in everyone. [When you murdered our grandmother, you killed] our matriarch, my best friend, my confidant, the woman who loved me (and everyone) unconditionally. I lost my hero that night and I lost her in the most horrible way imaginable.

Then the tone of her letter suddenly changed:

The internal struggle that has eaten me alive all these years has to end . . . now. I am tired, Jimmy. I am tired. I am tired of carrying this pain, hate, and rage in my heart. I can't do it anymore. I have to do this and truly forgive you.

James was shocked to receive the letter. He expected the letter to be full of vengeance, but Sarah was ready to forgive James. This is how James responded to Sarah's letter:

Dear Sarah, receiving your letter was the single most edifying, uplifting moment that I have experienced, short of October 6, 2001, when I forced the county jail to be baptized for the remission of my sins into the death & resurrection of Jesus Christ . . . I know you didn't write the letter to hear me say 'I'm sorry,' Sarah, sorry could never come close to what is in my heart and soul. The self-loathing, shame, shock and utter disbelief at what took place at my hand almost overcame me. If not for God's grace I would be gone. I don't think I could tell you anything that would explain or enlighten. There is no explanation. I loved [your grandmother]. Loved her with all my heart. Still do.

---

66. Bruce Springsteen, "Letter to You," 2020, Sony/ATV Publishing.

So James turned to God soon after he was incarcerated, and without God's grace, James felt that he would have taken his own life—he "would be gone." When Sarah received that letter from James, she felt all her hate and anger melt away. She felt free again for the first time in twenty long years. So both of them felt free. James felt her forgiveness, and Sarah felt his pain and sorrow for the crime he had committed. They talked by phone and developed a supportive relationship.

The story of James and Sarah is a story of reconciliation. Forgiveness is at the heart of reconciliation. Sarah's willingness to forgive changed everything for her and for the one she had hated for twenty years. Old things were done away; all things had become new. They were both made new creatures in Christ.

Now let's take this one step further. Let's consider the contribution Bruce Springsteen made in this story of reconciliation. He's a songwriter and performer who happened to write the song "Letter to You" precisely when Sarah needed to hear it. The song had recently been released when she heard it on the radio. Springsteen exerted significant compassionate imagination when he wrote the lyrics, and then Sarah exerted her own compassionate imagination as she listened to the lyrics.

Music brought the songwriter and the listener together. Then those lyrics caused the listener to write a letter of forgiveness that brought two people together who had been distanced from each other for twenty years. So much compassion. So much imagination. Sarah had to imagine how James would respond to the letter. She did not know if he would respond positively or throw the letter in the trash. James did not expect Sarah to forgive him, and he did not know how she would respond to his return letter. They both had to use compassionate imagination to embrace reconciliation. There was a little bit of *freudenfreude* going on. Sarah was rejoicing in being free from anger and hate, and James was rejoicing in his feelings of being forgiven for what he saw as his unforgivable crime. So they rejoiced together. This is the power of compassionate imagination.

The story of James and Sarah should give everyone hope that past sins can be swallowed up in the Savior's Atonement and that we can forgive each other even for what might seem unforgivable actions. We can forget the past and move imaginatively into the future. We can show compassion and leave anger, shame, and hate behind. Oneness with God and unity with others—this is how broken relationships can heal, and we can find peace in a fractured world.

CHAPTER 32
DISAGREE RESPECTFULLY

PRESIDENT NELSON RECENTLY OFFERED SIX SUGGESTIONS FOR RESPECT-fully disagreeing with each other. He drew these suggestions from the interaction he has with his presidency. One might ask, well, if all three in the First Presidency are prophets, seers, and revelators, why don't they always see things the same way? Why do they disagree with each other? There are lots of ways to answer this, but one way is to say that God works with His children in their uniqueness. And He does not make decisions for us, or He would be thwarting our agency. So we each receive inspiration a bit at a time in our own way, and as we receive it, we counsel together. This counseling process stems from the grand council in heaven. We do everything in the Church based on councils, including family councils. By definition, those participating in councils differ in how they see the same decision. We talk until we find common ground and come to unity.

Let's look at President Nelson's six suggestions:

1) Express feelings with love. My wife is good at this. I can be heading in a certain direction with a decision, and she can lead me in a different direction with a few words, spoken kindly—not making me feel like my direction is ridiculous. This means she has to listen to me, interpret me, and figure out why I'm thinking in a certain way. Sometimes, she can start a conversation like this: "This hasn't been my best day, and I can tell it hasn't been yours either." I totally agree, and then we talk until we figured out why it hadn't been so great. My reasons might be different than hers, but we come to understand each other. And it helps. If we didn't love each other, why would we care that the day had not been our best? So love is always at the base of our conversations.

2) Don't think you know best. This is a trap we all fall into at times. We've seen it in the workplace. One person gets their mind made up that something needs to happen in a certain way, and no amount of discussion will change the person's view. In a previous chapter, we called it rigidity, which can be destructive. Rigidity makes your brain turn off. It makes it impossible for you to listen to the other person. It shuts down conversation. Reasoning together stops. A friend once said some people are more interested in being certain than they are in being right. I once participated in a meeting at work where a very articulate group member laid out a case for moving in a certain direction on an issue. I think some group members were convinced that his approach made sense when he finished. But I had my doubts. I looked across the table and said, "That's a very compelling case, but I want to know, do you really believe that's the way we should go? He paused briefly and said, "Maybe I got a little carried away." We talked more and went in a very different direction with the decision.

3) Don't compete. Competition can be very attractive to some people. We can get wound up, trying to win our points simply because we want to win. But competition leads to winners and losers. And if someone loses the argument, relationships are often damaged. One person goes away feeling put down, rejected, and unappreciated.

4) Don't rigorously defend your position. Because we grow up thinking that competition is good, we often learn how to defend our position. We learn how to write persuasive essays, how to debate an issue in current events, and how to engage in political discourse. The French love debates. They love watching them on TV. They engage in debates in casual conversation. They like it when the debate gets heated. And Americans like to debate, too, even though we don't call it that. We call it political campaigning. We watch as candidates for political office rigorously defend their position and, in the process, attack their opponent by discounting their opponent's position. It's kind of like a verbal football game. We mount our offense and put on a strong defense. But this kind of conversation does not lead to stronger relationships. It certainly does not lead to Christlike unity.

5) Let the Spirit guide your conversations. In a good conversation, truth emerges, and each party feels better because both are open to the promptings of the Spirit. I don't think that this is usually a conscious thing. It just happens when we let God prevail. I was teaching a class recently, and some comments led us exactly where we needed to go. Following the class, as I reflected on how things happened, I could come to only one conclusion: the Spirit was guiding the discussion. At one point, one brother commented, and I jokingly said, "This brother was meant to be here today because he said exactly what needed to be said right at this moment. His comment leads us just where we need to go."

6) Be filled with charity, the pure love of Christ. Love is the key. Competition and rigidity can lead to abuse. But charity lifts everything upward. Everyone feels better following the discussion. No one feels ignored, left out, or devalued. Rather, everyone is edified. That doesn't mean that those who participate in the discussion always agree with each other. Different points of view can be enriching and enlivening. But when those present love one another, the journey to unity is uplifting, rejuvenating, and even thrilling.

These six suggestions by President Nelson are a formula to help us find Christlike unity with one another. Compassion underlies every one of the six suggestions. When we see things differently than someone else, our comments will always lead toward unity if we have compassion toward that person. The process of listening can be compassionate, and it also requires imagination. I call it perspective-taking. We must try to understand why the person sees the issues differently than we do. We must take the other person's perspective—see things through that person's eyes. That takes imagination, and it also takes compassion. When compassion and imagination come into play, unity will grow, and when Christlike unity with one another increases, oneness with God will follow.

The HEART Approach—R: Recognize the Hand of God

As mission leaders, we encouraged our missionaries to recognize the hand of the Lord every day. It worked. Missionaries would recount to us how they would feel divine guidance multiple times per day. The more they recognized His hand in their lives, the more success they found in their work. So it is with all of us: the more we acknowledge the Lord's power in our lives, the closer we feel to Him and to those around us. Recognizing His hand is an essential aspect of compassionate imagination. If we want to pursue a righteous goal, we must first imagine it, envision how we can achieve it, act in faith until we reach it, and recognize His hand—the Lord's divine help—as we work toward it.

Why don't we recognize His hand more often in our lives? I believe the distractions of the world get in our way. We imagine doing something important and then get interrupted by less worthy goals. As BYU-Pathway missionaries, we found that some students were desperately eager to find better employment—a worthy goal—but they had difficulty managing their time. Life often seemed to get in the way, so they set aside the assignment due that day to take care of a more pressing problem. During one of our online gathering meetings, one student, who was doing very well in the course, gave the following counsel to the other students:

> Hey, there's only one way to succeed in Pathway: to work on it every day first thing! You don't let one day go by without doing something on your assignments. You don't let anything else get in the way. You don't wait until the day before the assignment is due

to start working on it. And you don't wait until evening time. If you do, you'll never get your work done. First thing every single day! If you do this, God will help you get an *A* on every assignment. If you don't, you're on your own, and you won't succeed.

Students who were succeeding in their studies often mentioned how they would not be able to succeed without God's help. They recognized His hand often, just as our missionaries did. Those who did not succeed were less likely to say they felt God's help. This is such an important principle as we develop our compassion and imagination. Imagining success, especially when it seems unlikely, requires divine intervention. And the way to feel God's power in our lives more is to recognize His hand more often. That means we must focus on a righteous goal, as did the Pathway students who succeeded. We need to manage our time and avoid the distractions of the world.

CHAPTER 33

PAY ATTENTION, INCREASE DEVOTION

I SAW THIS PHRASE I LIKED THE OTHER DAY: ATTENTION IS THE BEGINning of devotion. We live in a world of distraction: notifications, ads, articles, headlines, and more all vie for our attention. When we're trying to get something important done, a notification sneaks on our screen and diverts us. So we try to turn off as many notifications as we can, but they still seem to keep coming, one after another. In one sense, they kidnap our brain and leave us wondering why we allowed a few pixels on a screen to take us hostage—to prevent us from doing the important thing we wanted to do.

Agency is related to attention. We choose what we will focus on. We choose to attend to someone fully or to let something in the background cause us to attend only halfway. At moments, distractions can be life-threatening. Some estimate that over 400 people die every year because the driver was texting. In addition, nearly 3,000 people die in accidents because of inattentive driving.[67] Texting is not the only thing that draws our attention away from the road. Our minds wander, and that can kill us and others in our path.

---

67. "Texting and Driving Accident and Death Statistics," *Miller & Zois*, 2024, https://www.millerandzois.com/car-accidents/more-accident-types-valuing-accidents/texting-and-driving-accident-and-death-statistics-2023-updated/.

What about distractions that lead us away from the Spirit? Thoughts that divert us, media, images, sounds—so many possible distractions. But when we let our minds take our attention off our spiritual journey, we run into the same problems as when we allow ourselves as drivers to take our eyes off the road. This is why agency, attention, and devotion go together. If we use our agency to focus on righteous goals and stay focused, just as our Pathway student counseled his classmates to do, we will see God's hand in our lives, our devotion to the Lord will increase, and we will achieve our purpose here on earth.

To experience unity in our relationships, we must also pay attention to our family members and friends. Studies have shown that 70% of parents feel distracted by their phone when they are caring for their children.[68] You can imagine the image of a child tugging on her mom's dress, but the mom doesn't notice because she's texting or reading something on her phone. Family therapists are seeing this as a serious problem—it's a type of child neglect. So we need to pay attention to family members if we want God's help raising our families.

When I was called as Sunday School General President, the General Authority Seventy who presided over our department at Church headquarters asked if I would come to his home and visit with him. That was a unique experience. I wondered what the visit would be like. He was a seasoned Church leader at the general level, and I was a novice. He welcomed me into his study in his home, got out a notepad, and said, "I just want to learn from you. If it's all right, I would like to ask you questions so I can learn." He then asked questions about learning and teaching because that was my charge as Sunday School General President. Our conversation was enriching in all sorts of ways. He asked penetrating questions, and I did my best to respond.

My wife asked me about the visit after I returned home. I said, "I don't think I have ever been with anyone in my life who is as good a listener as he was." I could still say that. Many people are eager to talk, but they fail to listen. I did not need to ask him to turn his phone off so he would pay attention to what I was saying. He was glued to me. And that surprised me because I felt he knew at least as much as I did about our topics. But he listened and took notes, lots of notes. He was focused. His

68. "Why Should Parents Limit Their Phone Use Around Their Kids?," *Psych Central*, https://psychcentral.com/lib/put-your-phone-away-and-pay-attention-to-your-kids.

ability to pay attention was a clear indication to me of devotion to the Lord. As I reflect on our conversation, I believe that one of his purposes in asking me to come to his home was so that he could get to know me better—so that we could establish a more meaningful relationship. I had known him before in other contexts, but not deeply. When we pay attention to one another, we nurture our relationship. And that conversation helped me feel closer to him as my leader.

The Lord is the best listener of all. He is never distracted. He never ignores us. He never pretends to pay attention when He's not. His devotion to us is sure. When He asked us to draw near to Him, it's a bit like my Priesthood leader asking me to come over for a visit. The Lord is always trying to get closer to us. He is always trying to nurture the relationship we have with Him. That's why every time we recognize His hand in our life, we are in essence feeling His love for us, His compassion for us. And the more we feel His compassion, the more we can imagine ourselves doing the work He wants us to do.

CHAPTER 34

APPRECIATE THE POWER OF HUMAN TOUCH

WHEN WE RECOGNIZE THE HAND OF GOD IN OUR LIFE, WE OFTEN SAY that "we were touched" or "our hearts were touched" as we felt the Spirit. It's a figurative phrase but has important implications for compassion and imagination. The scriptures say His arms can enfold us, and His hands are always outstretched, ready to welcome us. We don't feel His hands or arms, but the image is essential to understanding what it means to recognize His hand in our lives. Although we cannot touch His hand in this life, we can convey the spiritual strength He gives by touching others. Human touch can bring unity. Human touch can heal.

During one of my assignments as Sunday School General President, I had an encounter in Argentina that reminded me of the importance of human touch. Following an evening training meeting, a 50-year-old son and his 80-year-old father approached me. I discovered early in the meeting that the father was blind and that his son had come to assist him. As they approached me, the son grasped his father's hand and gently placed it on my left arm. The father then began to stroke my arm, moving his hand from my elbow to my wrist again and again. As he stroked my arm, he explained in his native Spanish, "¡Muchisimas Gracias!" (Thank you so much!), repeating the phrase with each stroke. I have never had someone thank me in such a demonstrative way. I not only sensed his gratitude, but I felt it deeply. He might have said, "Thanks for the training," as he passed me, but this was much more. Words alone can be powerful, but when combined with human touch, the message takes on a whole different dimension.

The pandemic of 2020 nearly eliminated human touch from our interactions with one another. There were moments when I felt a certain amount of both physical and emotional pain from not being able to give someone a hug or a kiss. The pandemic caused many people to experience "touch starvation." As Asim Shah of the Department of Psychiatry at Baylor College of Medicine has explained,

> Human beings are wired to touch and be touched. When a child is born, that is how they bond with their mother— through touch. Our wiring system has touch everywhere, so it's difficult for us not to think about physical contact. . . . When someone is [touch] starved, it's like someone who is starved for food . . . They want to eat, but they can't. Their psyche and their body want to touch someone, but they can't do it because of the fear associated with, in this case, the pandemic.[69]

Lolly: Just before serving as mission leaders twenty years ago, I was unexpectedly diagnosed with a small lump on my thyroid, which turned out to be cancer. The treatment involved surgery and then swallowing some radioactive liquid. This made me radioactive, and I had to isolate myself from my husband, my daughter, and her husband, who lived with us then. Because our daughter was pregnant, she and her husband stayed in a tent in the backyard as far away as possible in order to not endanger the unborn child. It's difficult to describe the feelings of isolation I felt. Yes, I could talk to family for a short time from a distance of at least ten feet, but it was the absence of actual hugs and touch that I craved the most. It made me feel crazy somehow. I had no physical pain, but life felt so empty and lonely.

I felt that same emptiness and loneliness when Russ and I had to suddenly return home from teaching in Hawaii. BYU Hawaii, The Polynesian Cultural Center, and the Laie Hawaii Temple closed overnight, and we

---

69. Shanley Pierce, "Touch Starvation is a Consequence of COVID-19's Physical Distancing," *Texas Medical Center News*, 15 May 2020, https://www.tmc.edu/news/2020/05/touch-starvation/.

were told to book a flight and leave as soon as possible. All students who could return to their countries were also sent home. It was an emotional time for all, not even being able to say goodbye at our last class. We resumed teaching the next week on Zoom with online instruction, but it wasn't the same. We seemed to lose that intangible connection that comes with in-person learning. We missed daily greeting our students at the door in the Aloha spirit and individually joking and connecting with them.

Most do not view touch as the most essential of our five senses. Sight and hearing are usually seen as much more important. So the question arises: How important is the sense of touch to our well-being? How often, for example, is touch mentioned in the scriptures? Multiple Latter-Day Saint artists have created moving images of Christ embracing children, youth, and adults. These paintings have often been inspired by scriptural images, such as in the New Testament when Christ asked that little children be brought to Him "that he should touch them" (Mark 10:13).

The scriptures are replete with examples showing the power of human touch and how Jesus touched people frequently when he was here on earth. For example, touch often played a role in the way he healed his followers: "He touched her hand, and the fever left" (Matthew 8:15). "If I may touch but his clothes, I shall be whole" (Mark 5:28). The scriptures also include scenes where devoted saints expressed their love for one another through a kiss: "(He) fell on his neck, and kissed him: and they wept" (Genesis 33:4). "He kissed all his brethren, and wept upon them" (Genesis 45:15). These verses show how integral human touch is for devoted followers of Christ. Unity comes as we express love to one another. Compassionate acts often involve touch. We lay on hands to give blessings. We hold babies in our hands when we give them a name.

I am confident that one day, we will embrace the Savior as some artists have depicted. Until then, I want to do all I can to recognize His hand in a spiritual sense. I want Him to touch the eyes of my understanding (Doctrine and Covenants 76:19). The Lord can figuratively touch our hearts and our eyes and our ears. And as we recognize those spiritual touches, we will naturally reach out to others in love. Those that we embrace, I believe, can feel the love of the Lord through us. A handshake, a pat on the shoulder, or a hug can bring a feeling of God's love to those in our circle of acquaintances. Compassion, often expressed through touch, can release our imagination to do good and great things. Recognizing His hand brings oneness with God. Embracing others brings unity; as oneness and Christlike unity increase, we will grow in our capacity to heal a fractured world.

CHAPTER 35

ACCEPT CHRIST'S INFINITE AND INTIMATE ATONEMENT

ON A SPRING DAY, AT THE AWKWARD AGE OF 14, I WANTED TO LEARN how to high jump. I would gaze at the bar during gym class, knowing I could conquer it. I cleared the bar on my first attempt, so I thought I was sure to clear it again after the coach raised it to the next level. Jogging toward the bar, I took the leap, knocked it from its perch, and stretched my arm out to break my fall. My arm broke my fall, but my left wrist also broke. At first, I felt no pain—I must have been in shock—but then I saw that my arm was no longer straight. My wrist was bent at the breakpoint, and when my coach saw it, he panicked, "Oh, you've broken your arm, you've really broken it! We've got to get you to the office!"

I waited for what seemed to be hours, but I'm sure it was only minutes for my mom to come and take me to the doctor. Once in his office, the doctor pulled out a syringe with the longest needle I'd ever seen. He explained that he needed to insert the needle into the broken bone to deaden the nerves around the break before setting the bone and straightening my arm. Just as he was preparing to jab me with the needle, I saw my mom standing in the open doorway. "Oh, honey," she said, "if I could trade places with you right now, I would."

My mother's message was one of love, but it was more than that. She had never broken her arm, but she had felt severe pain before, so she could imagine what I was feeling. We call this empathy, but it's much more than empathy when it happens between loved ones. I can empathize with someone I don't know—like when I witnessed a head-on collision. I was driving to work and saw two cars in an intersection—one trying to turn left, the other speeding straight ahead. When they crashed, the car making a left turn flipped upside down and flew across the street only a few feet away from me. The driver had her seatbelt on, and I could see she was still alive. I ran to the nearest door, asked to use their phone, and called 911. The ambulance sped to the scene and ejected the woman from the car, and paramedics began to examine her. She was going to be OK. I had never seen that woman before, but I empathized with her.

I am certain that the woman was grateful for my help, but because we did not know each other, I do not believe she felt that I had personally relieved her pain. When my mother expressed her desire to take my place in that doctor's office, I felt some relief from my pain because I knew my mother meant what she said—that she would take my place if possible, that she would rather feel the needle going into her arm than watch it poking into mine. Her compassion had a calming effect. Even her presence in the doorway was therapeutic. I still would have felt her healing influence if she had said nothing. Because my mom knew and loved me, her empathy was stronger than my empathy for the injured woman.

For most of my life, when I have thought of Christ's Atonement, I have tried to envision the pain He must have felt in the Garden of Gethsemane and on the cross. I've pictured Him paying the price for all the sins of everyone who has lived, who now lives, or whoever will live. I've seen an image in my mind of collective suffering, as if all sins were combined and then erased by the Savior's sacrifice. Now, I believe I'm seeing things differently and more clearly.

All sins are unique to the individual. One person's theft differs from another person's theft. Someone might steal money from a bank; another might steal a person's self-respect by mocking and rejecting them. And the pain that comes from each type of theft will vary dramatically—for both the one who commits the sin and the victim. Sin and suffering are unique to the individual. The Savior's suffering is also unique to each of us as His followers and, yes, as His children. When we take His name upon us, we are born of Him and become His sons and daughters (Mosiah 27:25).

Joseph Smith saw God the Father and His son, and God called Joseph by his name. We often point to this event to show that Heavenly Father not only knew Joseph's name but knows our names as well. But because we are His sons and daughters, He knows much more than our names. He knows how we feel at any moment, just as my mother knew how I felt in the doctor's office. He knows our pain, our questions, our perplexities, our confusion, and our suffering. The Prophet Isaiah taught that Jesus was "wounded for our transgressions, he was bruised for our iniquities" (Isaiah 53:5). I now like to read that verse, "He was wounded for my transgressions, He was bruised for my iniquities." My transgressions are unique to me and me alone. Christ's Atonement means He feels for me in my distress differently than He feels for someone else during their distress. Every child of God is different. Our spiritual and emotional qualities differ as much from one another as our physical appearances do.

Presiding Bishop Merrill J. Bateman once said: "The Savior's atonement in the garden and on the cross is intimate as well as infinite. Infinite in that it spans the eternities. Intimate in that the Savior felt each person's pains, sufferings, and sicknesses."[70] That means that the Lord knows us so intimately that He knows what we need at any given moment. He rejoices with us when we rejoice and suffers with us when we suffer—always in the exact way that will strengthen us and bring us closer to Him and His Father.

The word *intimate* has numerous meanings, but I like the definition in the Oxford English Dictionary: "close in acquaintance or association; closely connected by friendship, very familiar." I would like to modify that definition as we contemplate the power of Christ's Atonement. Rather than "closely connected by friendship," we would say, "oneness with God and Christlike unity with others." When we covenant with God, we develop oneness with Him in an infinitely powerful way. We are bound or attached to Him in a pure love that transcends all other

---

70. Merrill J. Bateman, *The Power to Heal from Within*, General Conference, The Church of Jesus Christ of Latter-day Saints, Apr. 1995, Gospel Library App.

forms of love, the love President Nelson called *hezed*[71]—the Hebrew word for covenantal love.

No one knows us as well as the Savior. He was sent to earth to save all of God's children. He understands us in ways that no one on earth can understand us. He has known us since we were spiritually begotten by Heavenly Parents—longer than anyone on earth has known us. So, the infinite quality of His Atonement describes how He has paid for every sin of every person and the degree to which He understands our uniqueness as one of His children. In this way, the Savior's Atonement is infinitely intimate.

Those who try to understand how people think, feel, and behave have long sought to describe the quality of human consciousness—the human quality that makes us different from one another. When we were spiritually begotten, we became conscious beings. We could spiritually and mentally experience our surroundings. We exercised our agency and consciously decided to follow Christ, come to earth, and experience mortality with all its rewards and trials.

I recently read the words of a neuroscientist who described how impossible it is to experience someone else's consciousness:

> Consciousness is about experience. It's internal, and it's private. You can make guesses about what is going on in somebody's mind, but you have no authority or capacity to know.[72]

He's right. We cannot know another's thoughts and feelings precisely. We have no capacity or authority to do that. The experience of the other person is uniquely theirs and theirs alone. But Christ does have the capacity and the authority to do that. He can know exactly how we feel—our desire and need at any moment. Suppose I'm experiencing severe nerve pain in my back. In that case, Christ understands that pain, not because he experienced that exact pain while in the flesh, but because he has experienced all pain, all suffering, and all joys vicariously for each of us. Because He knows me, He knows my pain.

---

71. Russell M. Nelson, "The Everlasting Covenant," *Liahona*, October 2022, https://www.churchofjesuschrist.org/study/liahona/2022/10/04-the-everlasting-covenant?lang=eng.

72. Olivia Gil de Bernabe, "I feel, therefore I am: Leading Neuroscientist António Damásio speaks on human consciousness," May 2023, https://dailynexus.com/2023-05011/i-feel-therefore-i-am-leading-neuroscientist-antonio-damasio-speaks-on-human-consciousness/.

In the parable of the lost sheep, we see how the shepherd knows his sheep by appearance and name and by the composite of all our characteristics as a son or daughter of God. The lone sheep that wandered off may have left the group to show his independence from the herd, and the shepherd knew that. Likewise, in the parable of the prodigal son, the father probably knew that his son would squander his inheritance. Still, he knew that his son needed to exercise agency so that he could learn from his experience. The son's father had never eaten with pigs, but he could understand the son's struggle because he knew his son.

Whether we're experiencing nerve pain in our back or feeling lost and forgotten because we made a bad decision, the Lord knows how we feel. He knows our pain because He knows us as no one else can. His infinite love and intimacy are always waiting for us, just as the father was waiting for his wayward son to return home. All we need to do is move in the right direction. All we need to do is try, and His arms open wide to us, welcoming us back from a detour we have taken. I envision the prodigal son seeing his father in the distance, running to greet him, and the son falling to his knees out of gratitude and shock that his father still loves him. Then, when the father comes closer, he kneels next to his son, lowering himself to his son's level; their eyes meet as if they can see inside each other's hearts, and then they embrace and kiss—infinite love, infinitely intimate. We need to recognize His hand as the hand that heals, forgives, and strengthens us as unique individuals.

When I saw my mother in the open doorway, as the doctor was about to stick a needle in my arm, the sight of her alone was comforting, but then she said, "If I could trade places with you right now, I would." Her words and presence combined to remove my fear and reduce my pain. She taught me something of eternal significance, even though neither of us at the time fully understood the lesson. She taught me that the Savior knows us, is always waiting in an open doorway, and will help us overcome every trial we will ever face. He will lower himself to our level and see into our eyes. He will embrace us as no one else can—all because His love is infinitely intimate.

My witness is similar to Alma's when he testified:

Now the Spirit knoweth all things; nevertheless the Son of God suffereth according to the flesh that he might take upon him the sins of his people, that he might blot out their transgressions according to the power of his deliverance; and now behold, this is the testimony which is in me (Alma 7:13).

CHAPTER 36
NEVER FALL AWAY

I WANT TO DEAL WITH A SENSITIVE TOPIC IN THIS CHAPTER THAT AFFECTS everyone. It's sensitive because it's an issue that's emotional as well as spiritual. Nearly everyone knows at least one person who has at one time been active in the church and then decided to leave. Those close to the person who leaves often keep asking themselves, why? What happened? I thought they were devoted to God and to the Church, and then one day they say they're leaving. Do they still believe in God? The answer is that some do and some don't. It seems that they are faithful one day and faithless the next. This has much to do with recognizing God's hand every day.

From the very beginning of Christ's Church on the earth, some members have struggled to keep their faith. When Jesus made it clear to His listeners that He was God's son, some of His followers could not accept it. They may have seen Him as a great teacher, even a prophet— but the son of God? That was too much for them. In John 6:60, we read, "Many therefore of His disciples, when they had heard this, said, This is an hard saying; who can hear it?" These were not His detractors. These were His disciples, those close to him, those who loved His teachings— but they could not accept Him as God's only begotten son.

When I was a young man, I knew that a few of my peers left the Church, but we didn't talk about it much. Now, we hear it mentioned all too frequently. Are all the young people leaving the Church? Are Millennials all checking out? Are the Gen Z youth all apostatizing? I have reviewed some of the research that has been done to find out exactly how many are leaving. The research is not totally clear because it is not a simple matter to track every member of the Church. We have good data on how many new converts remain active; that percentage has not changed significantly over the years. Some wonder if we're losing more than we're baptizing, and we're definitely not. Some wonder if more new members come from new births than from convert baptisms, and they don't. We baptize nearly twice as many new converts compared with the number of new births in a year.[73]

I recently heard a general authority say that if we look at the numbers historically, the percent of members who leave the church has not increased. Some have determined that the percentage is even lower today than it was in the days of the early 1800s. Apostasy has always been a part of The Church of Jesus Christ. Members apostatized when Jesus walked on the earth; they apostatized in the early days of the Church, and some still choose to leave today. We must remember that nine of the original Twelve called by the Prophet Joseph left the Church, and apostasy continues today.

Here's the big difference. In the 1800s, there were fewer members of the Church than there are today, and those who left the Church could not broadcast their departure nearly as easily as people can today. There was no social media in the 1800s. It was usually a private decision that often stayed quite private. Now, we might hear of someone leaving and conclude that a large percentage are leaving when, in fact, most are remaining faithful. However, this doesn't take away the sting when loved ones turn away from their faith and God.

When Jesus proclaimed His divine sonship, He asked the Twelve if they were going away also. Simon Peter answered, "Lord, to whom shall we go? thou hast the words of eternal life. And we believe and are sure that thou art that Christ, the Son of the living God" (John 6:67–69).

If I had been there on that day, I would say this if Jesus asked us about my belief in Him: "[I] believe and [am] sure that thou art that Christ, the Son of the living God." This is what I want my children and grandchildren to say. That's what I want all new members of the Church to say, because if we can say this with all our heart, we will stay true. Like Peter, if we cannot say this, where would we go? Whom would we

---

73. "Growth of the Church of Jesus Christ of Latter-day Saints," Church Growth Blog Spot, 2023, http://ldschurchgrowth.blogspot.com/2023/04/2022-statisical-report.html.

worship instead of Christ? He is the aim of our devotion. It is His hand that we seek to recognize every day.

When Lolly and I were serving as mission leaders, President Boyd K. Packer said, "Brothers and sisters, don't worry about those newly baptized—they can be like the Lamanites who joined the Church long ago. They can be among those who never fell away" (Boyd K. Packer, personal communication, June, 2005). Then he quoted from Alma 23:6:

> I say unto you, as the Lord liveth, as many of the Lamanites as believed in their preaching, and were converted unto the Lord, never did fall away.

Every missionary worries about newly baptized members falling away, so Elder Packer's words came as a source of strength and comfort. But the words in this verse mean something different to me now. Notice the word *converted* in the verse. "As many of the Lamanites as believed in their preaching, and were converted unto of the Lord, never did fall away." I once thought that "converted" here meant "baptized and confirmed." But now I see it differently. It wasn't enough to simply "believe in their preaching." They had to be truly converted to the Lord. And conversion is not instant; it's a lifelong process.

Elder Christofferson discussed the scene in Mosiah when King Benjamin preached the word, and his listeners had no more disposition to do evil but to do good continually. Elder Christofferson explained that their change of heart did not come instantly. It took time.[74] I believe that is the same with the Lamanites' conversion. It took time. But the deeper the truth of the gospel sank into their hearts, the less inclination they had to depart from the faith they had embraced.

We experience conversion whenever we recognize God's hand or influence in our lives. We experience conversion when we see the effects of the gospel in someone else's life. Those who witnessed the Savior's miracles when He was here on the earth experienced an increase of faith, a deeper conversion, every time they witnessed it. But to experience that deeper witness, they had to first profess their belief in Him as the Son of God. Others saw the miracles and wrote them off as magic or coincidence. So we first accept the Lord as our Savior and Redeemer, and then

---

74. D. Todd Christofferson, *Born Again*, General Conference, The Church of Jesus Christ of Latter-day Saints, Apr. 2008, Gospel Library App.

we live in ways that allow us to grow in faith and surety that God is in the heavens and will help us along our way in mortality.

All of this implies that when we see someone lose their faith and leave the Church, we embrace them, love them, and have faith that they will one day return. We imagine their return with compassion. That is not only my hope, but it is my firm belief—that those who have professed a belief in the past will one day rediscover the truths that they once treasured, that the brightness of their belief will be reignited and grow inside them, that they will be so firmly converted that they will never fall away again.

I've mentioned that I have a brother who was less active for 30 years, and my wife has a brother who was less active for 50 years, but they have both come back into full activity in the Church. They both show that losing faith is often a temporary event. It does not define someone's life. The past can be put away. As the scripture says, "All things are become new" (2 Corinthians 5:17). And in the end, our present condition is all that matters. So if someone you love no longer feels close to the Church, my heart goes out to you. My prayer is that your loved ones will remember the faith that was once inside them and have a desire to return, as our brothers have done, because the process of conversion took hold. Even though they will have been distant for a time, they will come back, and so in a real sense, "They never did fall away."

CHAPTER 37
LET CHRIST'S ATONEMENT FREE YOU

To take full advantage of the Savior's Atonement, we need to recognize His hand continually. When we acknowledge His influence in our lives, we are more able to experience the infinitely intimate power of His sacrifice for us. Nicodemus is such an interesting example of a believer who came to know the Savior and believe in Him. I have always been fascinated by the story of Nicodemus. He is mentioned only by John, and only in three brief passages. Some Bible scholars conclude that Nicodemus never really believed that Jesus was the Messiah, while others conclude that he was. I side with those who see Nicodemus as one who was truly converted and became a faithful follower of Jesus.

Nicodemus was a Pharisee. The Pharisees focused on the outward expressions of faith rather than on the heart. Unlike the Sadducees, they believed in an afterlife, but held strictly to the law of Moses, so Jesus with His revolutionary teachings did not sit well with them. They were among Jesus's most vocal critics. So Nicodemus was an anomaly; that's likely why he met Jesus at night, so none of his fellow Pharisees would see him.

The beginning verses of John 3 are well known. Nicodemus approaches Jesus and says, "Thou art a teacher come from God." Nicodemus is trying to figure out just who Jesus is. He is saying, in essence, "I've heard of your miracles, and no ordinary man could perform such miracles, so I know you must be more than just another preacher. You must have come straight from God."

Then Jesus invites Nicodemus to be baptized by water and by the Holy Ghost. He explains that Nicodemus must be born again. This is all very perplexing to Nicodemus. He is taking everything literally and can't quite grasp what Jesus is trying to teach him, but that was how many of Christ's disciples reacted to His teachings—they simply did not understand at first.

Jesus taught Nicodemus as we should all teach one another. He responded to Nicodemus's questions. Jesus didn't lecture him. He taught him in a conversational way, one question at a time. The questions Nicodemus had were deeply personal for him. He was desperate to understand who Jesus really was. Later in John 7:51, Nicodemus appears to defend Jesus to the naysayers, many of whom were fellow Pharisees. And as Nicodemus was defending Jesus, he took a lot of heat from those around him.

Then in John 19:39, John refers to Nicodemus again: "And there came also Nicodemus, which at first came to Jesus by night, and brought a mixture of myrrh and aloes, about an hundred pound weight. Then took they the body of Jesus, and wound it in linen clothes with the spices, as the manner of the Jews is to bury."

So Nicodemus helped dress Jesus for burial. I don't believe that he would have done that unless he had come to believe in the divinity of Jesus. At some point, and we're not sure when, he came to know that Jesus was the Messiah, the son of God. As Jesus was responding to the questions of Nicodemus, he ended with what has become, perhaps, the most oft-quoted verse of all of scripture—John 3:16–17: "For God so loved the world, that he gave his only begotten Son, that whosoever believeth in him should not perish, but have everlasting life. For God sent not his son into the world to condemn the world, but that the world through him might be saved."

When Nicodemus said, "Thou art a teacher come from God," Jesus essentially responded, "Yes, God sent me here to earth, his Only Begotten son, so that I could redeem all of God's children—including you, Nicodemus."

Some have said that John 3:16–17 encapsulates the entire gospel of Jesus Christ. These few sacred words show us the nature of God: that God the Father is a separate being from His Son, and that His Son came to earth to bring salvation to anyone who would believe on His name—and with the verses that preceded, being baptized by both water and the

Holy Ghost. This is the doctrine of Christ: words that bring more hope, more joy to mortal beings than perhaps any other words.

When my wife and I were serving as temple president and matron of the Bismarck, North Dakota Temple, a member of the Seventy came to visit us in the summer of 2015. He and his wife sat across the table from us. The following is a summary of what he said:

> During April conference, I was sitting behind the podium so I could see the teleprompter quite clearly, so I followed along as President Packer gave his talk. His voice was weak, but I wanted to get every word he was saying, so I kept following along on the teleprompter. At the end of the talk, he left the words on the prompter and began to speak from his heart. Elder Packer looked up, and then he said:
>
> I am so grateful for the blessings of the Lord Jesus Christ, for the power of procreation, for the power of redemption, for the Atonement—the Atonement which can wash clean every stain no matter how difficult or how long or how many times repeated. The Atonement can put you free again to move forward, cleanly and worthy, to pursue that path you have chosen in life.
>
> I bear witness that God lives, that Jesus is the Christ, that the Atonement is not a general thing that is for the whole church. The Atonement is individual, and if you have something that is bothering you—sometimes so long ago you can hardly remember it—put the Atonement to work. It will clean it up, and you, as does He, will remember your sins no more.[75]

We didn't know at the time that those words would be the last President Packer would ever speak over the podium. That was April 2015, and he passed away that July. After I heard those words, I asked my wife to help me print those words and frame them. I wanted to look at them every day. They exemplify the profound meaning of the words in John 3:16–17. This is the exulting principle of the Savior's Atonement that Jesus was teaching Nicodemus. And it is the same exulting principal that President Packer shared in his final address to the Saints. I truly believe, as did President Packer, that Christ's Atonement can wash every stain and set us free to move forward, cleanly, and worthily to pursue our chosen path. How grateful I am for that knowledge for my own life, the life of my family, and the lives of all of God's children.

---

75. Boyd K. Packer, *The Plan of Happiness*, General Conference, The Church of Jesus Christ of Latter-day Saints, Apr. 2015, Gospel Library App.

The HEART Approach—T: Thank the Lord for His Blessings

I REMEMBER WATCHING PRESIDENT NELSON'S VIDEO ON GRATITUDE IN 2020 during some of the darkest, most troubling days of the pandemic—when many of us were at our lowest emotional point. At that time, most were focusing on the limitations the pandemic had forced on us. At that time, I remember feeling very hemmed in, cut off from many things that brought me joy. And here was President Nelson pleading with us to show gratitude for our blessings.

His video was powerful then and impressed me even more as I watched it again. If you have not watched that video recently, I urge you to take a look. It's powerful! After watching it, I could not help but reflect on all the blessings I enjoy—one of which is the blessing of a living prophet. At the end of the video, President Nelson prays. We seldom hear a prophet appealing directly to heaven in prayer. In general conference, prayers are always given by other Church leaders, never the prophet himself. And his prayer in this video will lift and inspire anyone who listens with an open heart.

The video lasts nine minutes. It may be the best nine minutes you spend today. And if you've already watched it, I'm convinced that viewing it again will be well worth it. President Nelson mentions how the power of gratitude has been shown by both science and in the Scriptures to have positive effects, but more powerful than anything that has been said in the past are the words of a living prophet—God's mouthpiece on earth. President Nelson was speaking not only to members of our church but to the whole world. The video has had over 65 million views.

Giving thanks is an essential component of compassionate imagination. Gratitude makes us more generous, compassionate, and optimistic. It fuels our imagination because as gratitude grows inside us, it helps us feel more capable, more lovable, and more able to meet the demands of life. It causes us to focus on the positive and shifts our minds away from the troubles, worries, and tragedies we witness in the world. It is a Godly quality. It brings us closer to God, so it helps us hear Him. It brings unity because our feelings of gratitude often center on our families and friends. Gratitude can have a miraculous healing influence on us every day. That is perhaps why President Nelson made that video in the deepest, most difficult part of the pandemic. He knew that if we could feel gratitude, we would feel God's love for us, and if we felt God's love for us, we would have compassion for all His children. Gratitude sparks our imagination for a better world where peace and acceptance of belonging prevail.

CHAPTER 38
GIVE THANKS AND BE FULLY PRESENT

POSITIVE PSYCHOLOGISTS OFTEN FOCUS ON THE IMPORTANCE OF GRATI-
tude in our lives. They also emphasize how essential it is for us to be fully
present.

Lolly: Just before the pandemic, we served seven months as missionaries where we team taught religion at BYU Hawaii. Early in the semester, we encouraged our students to use their devices only for class purposes, such as scriptures or class activities involving a search of a gospel
topic. They needed their devices to take notes and look up things, but the
devices could easily distract them and others around them. We talked
about cell phone and computer use in class and decided that if they had
an emergency that couldn't wait, they should just leave the room so as
not to interrupt others and return when they could fully engage in the
class, being fully present.

This condition of being fully present and the disposition of gratitude go together. In this way, gratitude is more than a feeling, more
than a disposition; it's a state of being, and being fully present is also
a state of being. These are not conditions that we feel only in times of
prayer. They are our defining characteristics every day, no matter how

bad the day may have gone. We are still grateful, and we are still present. How can we exercise compassionate imagination if we are not fully present? Imagination is a unique cognitive act, and it demands our full commitment.

During a visit to Paris some years ago, I took a break one afternoon in the Luxembourg Gardens. A white gravel path provides room for joggers and walkers, and benches are strategically placed so that you can view the carefully groomed beds of flowers and shrubs. The beauty is almost overcoming—a green oasis in the middle of one of the busiest cities in the world. While resting for a few minutes on a bench, I noticed a mother and her son strolling along. Her son, about six years old, began peering up into the thick branches of the mammoth horse chestnut tree. His mother asked what he was looking at, and he pointed to the bird perched on a high branch: "Look, mama, that big mama bird is feeding her little birds!" The boy was genuinely excited, and the mother seemed equally excited, responding, "I've never actually seen a bird feed its young. You have such a good eye!"

The scene impressed me because the mother and her son were interacting in an almost magical way. The two of them sat on an adjoining bench so that they could keep watching and talking about the bird. The mother could've brushed off the son and asked him to hurry along to get where they were going. But she didn't. She enjoyed the show the bird was putting on as much as her son. And the moment allowed her to praise the son for his perceptiveness.

What did this scene teach me? The importance of being fully present. The mother and her son were present with each other. The son's observation of the bird led to the mother's observation. She was not checking her messages. Neither of them was thinking about yesterday, last year, or the future. They were in the here and now. We all need to live in the present, to drink it in with all of its unpredictability and absorb all that it has to offer.

A conversation, like the one between the mother and son in the Luxembourg Gardens, is spontaneous. Neither participant in the conversation knows where it will lead. I did not stay long enough to see where the mother and son went next or how they continued their observations. One of the wonders of how relationships are made is being open to the flow of comments that one cannot predict. The son was somewhat surprised that his mother had never seen a mama bird feed its young.

That was one of the reasons he took such delight in her reaction. She was learning along with him. She was experiencing newness at the same time he was experiencing it. Fully present, simple, unpredictable, and enlightening. Compassion was part of their encounter, and so was imagination.

Technology has made being fully present more challenging for everyone with a cell phone, computer, or television. As much as these devices have enriched our lives, they have also distracted us from the here and now. Whether texting while driving or looking at our phone when someone else is talking to us, how different that scene in the park would have been if the mother had pulled her phone from her purse and began texting a friend while her son was trying to get her attention. But she didn't. Rather, she gave all her consciousness to him, not because she reluctantly tore herself away from what she wanted to do at the moment, but because she wanted to do what he wanted to do. That's compassionate imagination. Again, so fully present, so simple, so unpredictable, so enlightening.

Lolly: Russ's experience watching that mother and her son reminded me how important it is to be grateful for God's creations. I was studying a talk by President Nelson given in April of 1990. He was talking about the importance of using the correct name of our Church. He gave that talk over 30 years ago, and I hope with his latest reiteration about gratitude as our Prophet, we, as a Church, are coming to understand the will of the Lord. I felt true inspiration speaking to my soul as Elder Nelson talked about what it means to be a Saint. One gem stood out to me. Maybe because I was alone, looking out over the valley where I live, I heard this in my heart: "A Saint is reverent. We must have reverence for the Lord, for the earth he created."[76] It was on one of those "be-still-my-soul, the-Lord-is-on-thy-side" moments. I prayed that I might have taught this to my children.

One way I hopefully cemented this important doctrine of being reverent for God's creations was Primary Music time. I had ample opportunities to teach the gospel through music throughout my life. Russ and I were even co-Primary music leaders together for a short time. As you

---

76. Russell M. Nelson, *"Thus Shall My Church Be Called,"* General Conference, The Church of Jesus Christ of Latter-day Saints, Apr. 1990, Gospel Library App.

may know, young children need many ways to keep them focused, so we tried to keep their hands, bodies, ears, eyes, and voices involved.

A favorite of mine, "My Heavenly Father Loves Me," was so descriptive of what I think reverence for the Lord and for the earth he created means. It was easy to express the words with hand movements or simple signs.

> Whenever I hear the song of a bird
> Or look at the blue, blue sky,
> Whenever I feel the rain on my face
> Or the wind as it rushes by,
> Whenever I touch a velvet rose
> Or walk by our lilac tree,
> I'm glad that I live in this beautiful world
> Heav'nly Father created for me (Children's Songbook, p. 228).

Simple actions for the children always held them attentive while we sang the tender words to the song. I wanted the children to know the words in their hearts so the memory would be there years later to remind them to always be grateful for this beautiful earth that Heavenly Father created for them.

Elder Uchtdorf reminds us that we not only need to be grateful for things when life is going our way but also in all our circumstances, whatever they are. He asks, "Could I suggest that we see gratitude as a disposition, a way of life that stands independent of our current situation? . . . We can choose to be grateful no matter what."[77]

The simple thought of always having a reverent attitude for God's creations can help us develop this disposition of gratitude. A child's natural wonderment for beauty needs to be nourished, and music is one way to superglue the thought of reverence for God's creations in the hearts and minds of our young.

---

77. Dieter F. Uchtdorf, *Grateful in Any Circumstances*, General Conference, The Church of Jesus Christ of Latter-day Saints, Apr. 2014, Gospel Library App.

CHAPTER 39
CURE LONELINESS

THE SURGEON GENERAL, DR. VIVEK MURTHY, RECENTLY SENT AN 81-page report to the government about our most pressing health problem in the United States. Was it a report on cancer? Heart disease? Diabetes? Long COVID? No. It was on the epidemic of loneliness. This emotional problem contributes to every physical ailment you can think of. That is why loneliness is costing the healthcare industry billions of dollars annually. Murthy said that about half of the population say they've experienced loneliness.

> "We now know that loneliness is a common feeling that many people experience. It's like hunger or thirst. It's a feeling the body sends us when something we need for survival is missing. Millions of people in America are struggling in the shadows, and that's not right. That's why I issued this advisory to pull back the curtain on a struggle that too many people are experiencing."
>
> Research shows that Americans, who have been less engaged with worship houses, community organizations and even with their own family members in recent decades, have steadily reported an increase in feelings of loneliness. The number of single households has also doubled over the past 60 years.[78]

This book is about finding oneness and Christlike unity in a fractured world. Nothing is more convincing that the world is fractured than these data. As Murthy says, families are fractured, churches are

---

78. Amanda Seitz, "Loneliness Poses Risks as Deadly as Smoking: Surgeon General," *AP News*, May 2, 2023.

fractured, and neighborhoods are fractured. "Wars and rumors of wars" are the strongest evidence of a fractured world. But those are often distant from us. Loneliness is in our backyard or even within the walls of our own homes. These are the fractures we can work on most readily, and the work we need to do requires immense compassion and imagination. We need to imagine fractured relationships healing. We need to imagine past offenses evaporating. For those things to happen, we need more imagination, creativity, optimism, faith, and compassion than ever.

The thing I find fascinating about the surgeon general's report is that our country is now recognizing the underlying causes of our health problems. He could very easily focus on the problem of type two diabetes or cancer or heart disease—all of which take the lives of millions of people every year. But he's looking deeper. He's looking at what could be the most powerful contributing factor to our overall health: relationships. The life span of lonely people is 30% shorter than those who are not lonely.[79] And the epidemic of loneliness is hitting our youth particularly hard. Of course, lonely people are likely to experience anxiety and depression at higher rates than those who are not lonely. We don't need more research to show the negative effects of this epidemic. We see the effects every day.

When the Lord instructs us to "meet together oft" (Moroni 6:6) as He did to the Nephites, He means what He says. I've heard many people joke about how Latter-day Saints know how to do one thing very well: "meet together often." We know how to call meetings and attend them—ward council, stake council, youth council, family council—you name it, we have a meeting for it. These meetings serve many purposes— one of which is to help everyone feel included so that no one is left out. The central purpose of ministering is to erase loneliness to help everyone feel the fellowship of ward friends.

Lolly and I once visited our kids who live in Puerto Rico. On Sunday, I attended the priests quorum with my grandson, who conducted the meeting and taught the lesson. He focused on the fifth article of faith: "We believe that a man must be called of God, by prophecy, and by the laying on of hands by those who are in authority, to preach the gospel

---

79. Linda Searing, "Does loneliness affect lifespan?," *The Washington Post*, 2015, https://www.washingtonpost.com/national/health-science/does-loneliness-affect-life-span/2015/03/30/b5d112c6-d3ea-11e4-ab77-9646eea6a4c7_story.html.

and administer the ordinances thereof." As he directed the lesson, he asked each young man to click on a link in the verse and describe how that principle related to receiving a calling. So one of the priests clicked on *prophecy*, leading him to the topical guide with verses about that word. My grandson then asked him to share with the group how prophecy related to receiving a calling in the Church. One by one, all participated repeatedly. No one was left out. No one felt ignored or forgotten. All felt equally needed. There were moments of laughter, moments of insight, and moments of spiritual uplift. It reminded me of the verse in the Doctrine and Covenants: "That all may be edified of all" (Doctrine and Covenants 88:122).

So when the surgeon general says there is no substitute for face-to-face interaction, he's serious. We are commanded to meet together oft so that all can be edified of all. There is an inborn human need to be with others to show and receive love. When the prodigal son returned, his father fell on his neck and kissed him; he was so overjoyed to see his son again, face-to-face. His son had been lost, but now he was found. He was lonely no longer. The father's compassion is the kind of compassion everyone needs, and we must do all we can to see that those in our circle are receiving it. Elder Holland once spoke of the loneliness of the Savior felt as He gave his life for us. No one in human history had ever felt more alone than Jesus did on that cross. As Elder Holland said:

> Because Jesus walked such a long, lonely path utterly alone, *we* do not have to do so. His solitary journey brought great company for our little version of that path—the merciful care of our Father in Heaven, the unfailing companionship of His beloved son, the consummate gift of the Holy Ghost, angels in heaven, family members on both sides of the veil, prophets and apostles, teachers, leaders, friends. All of these and more have been given as companions for our mortal journey, because of the Atonement of Jesus Christ and the Restoration of His gospel. Trumpeted from the summit of Calvary is the truth that we will never be left alone nor unaided, even if sometimes we may feel that we are. Truly the Redeemer of us all said: "I will not leave you comfortless: [My Father and] I will come to you [and abide with you]."[80]

---

80. Jeffrey R. Holland, *None Were with Him*, General Conference, The Church of Jesus Christ of Latter-day Saints, Apr. 2009, Gospel Library App.

Elder Holland is helping us understand that we will never be lonely if we stay close to the Lord. And when loneliness strikes as it does for most people at some point in their lives, we can turn to the one who knows more about loneliness than anyone else: our Savior, Jesus Christ. He promised that He would be with us, and He never breaks a promise. We are His covenant children. We are bound to Him and He to us. And the closer we draw to Him, the closer we will draw to those around us, our family and friends. Our attachment to the Lord is more important than any other relationship. I hope you will do all you can to draw near unto Him. And then you will naturally reach out to others so that no one is left out. This is the one sure way to conquer the epidemic of loneliness that plagues the world. The solution begins with our closeness to God. He is the endless source of compassionate imagination.

CHAPTER 40

EXPERIENCE
EVERYDAY GRACE

WE NEED TO THANK GOD FOR HIS GRACE EVERY DAY. GOD IS "THE Father of mercies, and the God of all comfort" (2 Corinthians 1:3). What was His most compassionate act? Allowing His Son to save us from the pain of mortality. Compassion from the Father and then compassion from the Son to us. So, as we feel compassion from both the Father and the Son, we let Their compassion flow through us to others. It is like a never-ending stream of pure divine love that we receive from them and give to those around us. This is the essence of God's grace, and the more we imagine Their grace flowing into us and through us, the more that grace will comfort and strengthen and bring Christlike unity to the world.

The scriptures tell us that Jesus was "declared to be the Son of God with power, according to the spirit of holiness . . . by whom we have received grace" (Romans 1:4–5). Only a few words, but so powerful!

God's grace is more far-reaching than anyone can imagine. By grace, we exist. By grace, He gave birth to our spirit. By grace, we breathe and have our being in mortality. By grace, we were given the precious gift of agency—the power to direct our own lives without coercion, force, or manipulation. By grace, we will one day be resurrected and perfected in Him.

When we take on a new challenge, it is by grace that we accomplish what first seemed impossible. When we are discouraged, it is by grace that we regain our sense of purpose and meaning. By the Lord's grace, we hope, we love, we reach out to others. By grace, we learn and grow and change.

Yes, the power of God's grace is more magnificent than any word or phrase can define. By grace, the world was created. The trees, mountains, and streams show evidence of the Savior's grace.

So my question is: Why don't we recognize His grace more often and with more gratitude? Why do we forget so easily that by grace, we are healed? Why do we sometimes feel like we are going it alone—that our own strength is all we have? Why do we not draw upon His grace more often? Experiencing God's grace can be an everyday experience. We need only to open ourselves to it.

The world denies God's grace. The world emphasizes the tangible and ignores the ineffable. If we can't touch it, smell it, taste it, or hear it, it doesn't exist. But we do not touch, smell, taste, or hear grace. Grace is a force that enters our whole being. Sometimes, it enters without our invitation, surprising us by its presence. Other times, it comes only after our pleas for help—following prayer and fasting. God's grace is our life-blood. The power enables us to keep going when the odds are against us.

I recently read a story about Joel Sonnenberg, who, at the age of 22 months, was involved in a devastating accident that left him with burns over 85% of his body. Sonnenberg was burned after a tractor-trailer crashed into the car he was riding in, resulting in the rupturing of its fuel tank. Little Joel was rescued from the burning car by a stranger. The tissue damage included the loss of the fingers on his right hand, his entire left hand, and his ears, as well as damage to his skull.

It took Sonnenberg many years to recover from the burn injuries. He endured 45 surgeries and the emotional pain of dealing with disfigurement. Still, through his faith, family, and friends, he became a student leader, all-conference athlete, and internationally sought-after speaker.[81]

Reginald Dort drove the vehicle that crashed into the car Sonnenberg was in, and Dort skipped bail and kept driving for the next 18 years. Sonnenberg's mother felt that Dort should be in jail for what he did,

---

81. Holly Ramer, "Burned Baby Now a 'Diamond of Sparkling Beauty' as Adult," *Los Angeles Times*, August 23, 1998, https://www.latimes.com/archives/la-xpm-1998-aug-23-mn-15709-story.html.

but Sonnenberg forgave him and did not want to see him punished. The Sonnenberg and Dort story is similar to the Sarah and James story in a previous chapter. Sonnenberg might have hated Dort all his life, but he didn't. At Dort's sentencing, Sonnenberg forgave Dort and expressed his belief in the power of grace to heal Dort, as well as to heal his own wounds.

Sonnenberg could have been vindictive, but he wasn't, and he acknowledged the power that allowed him to forgive the one who caused him so much harm. Grace. Simply God's grace. He recognized that grace has no limits. It can heal any wound, physical or emotional. It can give us life when we feel like dying. It can lift us up when we fall down.

The stories of James killing Sarah's grandmother that we recounted in an earlier chapter and Joel Sonnenberg's story are all about everyday grace—the strengthening power that we can feel from God every day. We need to remember that God is the "Father of mercies, and the God of all comfort" and that His greatest gift to us was His son, who is equally full of compassion. I like to imagine compassion flowing into us—especially in times of trial and challenge. The more we see and feel God's compassion, the more we want to share it with others. Maybe this is what is meant by the phrase, "peace like a river." The water in the river flows from God the Father to His son, and if we see it and feel it, it keeps flowing through us to those we love. The more this happens in our lives, the more we will be ready for the second coming.

We all await the day when the Savior will return to the earth. Isaiah saw this day and said, "How beautiful upon the mountains are the feet of him that bringeth good tidings, that publisheth peace" (Isaiah 52:7). Enoch also saw in vision the second coming of the Savior. He saw that the Lord would descend, that all the righteous would be gathered from every corner of the earth and that the gathering place would be called Zion.

> And the Lord said unto Enoch: Then shalt thou and all thy city meet them there, and we will receive them into our bosom, and they shall see us; and we will fall upon their necks, and they shall fall upon our necks, and we will kiss each other (Moses 7:63).

I cannot conceive of a more joyous moment than Christ and those in the City of Enoch greeting the righteous Saints rising from their graves. This scene depicts the culmination of God's plan for His children from the time of Adam and Eve to this, the final dispensation when the fullness of the gospel has spread throughout the earth. It is an image of oneness with God and Christlike unity. Keeping this image in our mind and heart will ready us to greet Him on that great Millennial Day.

AFTERWORD

SOME ASK, "SO HOW LONG HAS IT TAKEN YOU TO WRITE THIS BOOK?" That's a hard question to answer. I could say, "Well, I've been thinking about this topic for the past ten years, and Lolly and I have discussed the topic from every possible angle." Was I writing much about it when I began thinking about it? Maybe a little bit, but not much. It took shape over time. The topic of imagination itself has intrigued us for years. It is one of the most magical of all human capabilities. Animals don't imagine things—at least not in the wide-ranging way humans do. So why do we not discuss this powerful human gift in the Church more often? Is it because the scriptures frequently mention the negative aspects of imagination, i.e., "vain imaginations"? But a verse in the Doctrine and Covenants describes how positive and uplifting imagination can be. The Lord was speaking through Joseph Smith to William Law and said: "And he shall be led in paths where the poisonous serpent cannot lay hold upon his heel, and he shall mount up in the imagination of his thoughts as upon eagles' wings" (Doctrine and Covenants 124:99).

I believe Joseph Smith understood the positive power of human imagination. The Lord didn't say "the imagination of God's thoughts"; he said the imagination of his (William Law's) thoughts. Human thoughts can be uplifting and even exalting when those thoughts are sparked by divine light. Immediately after the Church was organized in 1830, the prophet Joseph gathered with a few priesthood holders and held a meeting in which each bore testimony. After they had born witness of the Restoration, Joseph said something that surprised many of them:

Brethren, I have been very much edified and instructed in your testimonies here tonight, but I want to say to you before the Lord, that you know no more concerning the destinies of this Church and Kingdom than a babe upon its mother's lap. You don't comprehend it, it is only a little handful of Priesthood you see here tonight, but this Church will fill North and South America—it will fill the world.[82]

Before writing this book, I understood this expression by the prophet to mean that the others in the room did not have the same power to receive personal revelation that he did. After all, he was the prophet, and they were simply members of the new Church. I am not saying that such an interpretation is wrong, but we want to offer another possible way of understanding this quote. Joseph told them they were like "a babe upon its mother's lap." Some might see this pronouncement as condescending. We don't see it that way now. Babies have no imagination. They cannot think abstractly. Their cognitive capacity is extremely limited when they come into this world. So, we see Joseph's comment to be similar to the psychologist William James's statement mentioned earlier in the book when he said, "Unclamp your [brain] and let it run free; and the service it will do you will be twice as good."

I see Joseph's comment to those early church leaders as not condescending but instructive. He was trying to help them see that they could think more imaginatively if they would only allow themselves to do it. Their mental capacity was far greater than they realized, and if they nurtured their imaginative powers, they would see as Joseph had seen—that the Church would cover the whole earth.

Writing this book has helped me see that imagination is a spiritual gift. The word in French for spirit and mind is the same: *esprit*. We use this word in English when we say things like *esprit de corp*. Gifts of the Spirit draw upon the mind, the intellect. Consider the following list of spiritual gifts from the 46th section of the Doctrine and Covenants: the gift of tongues (speaking foreign languages), interpretation of tongues (understanding foreign languages), translation, knowledge, teaching, and wisdom. All these gifts of the Spirit require mental exertion. To acquire any of these gifts, we must use our imagination. We must envision ourselves being able to communicate in another language. We need

---

82. *Teachings of the Presidents of the Church: Joseph Smith* (Salt Lake City: The Church of Jesus Christ of Latter-day Saints, 2007), p.140-141.

to envision ourselves acquiring wisdom and knowledge. So, imagination is one of the keys to acquiring and exercising spiritual gifts. But not just any kind of imagination—compassionate imagination.

When I first began thinking about this book, I decided on the term "moral imagination," which is a good term. The opposite would be immoral imagination, which would lead us to commit evil acts. But I finally settled on "compassionate imagination" because this term, I believe, is the quality that Joseph was asking those early leaders to develop. Envisioning the Church as an organization that would one day cover the earth required an enormous leap of faith and imagination, but it also demanded compassion. What could be more compassionate than to help the Lord accomplish His mission "to bring to pass the immortality and eternal life of man?" So, we hope that something in this book will lead you to a little more imagination and a little more compassion. If so, we will have accomplished what we set out to do.

ABOUT THE AUTHORS

RUSSELL T. AND LOLA S. OSGUTHORPE ARE THE PARENTS OF FIVE CHIL-dren, 23 grandchildren, and three great children. Their posterity has been the prime focus of their lives. During their careers, they both served as educators, Russ at the National Technical Institute for the Deaf and Brigham Young University, and Lolly at Provo School District (Utah). Whether they were serving as teachers or church leaders, they have always focused on helping others reach their full potential. Russ served in various positions in The Church of Jesus Christ of Latter-day Saints, including Sunday School General President. Lolly has also served in leadership positions in the Church. Together they have served as mission leaders in the South Dakota Rapid City Mission, president and matron of the Bismarck North Dakota Temple, senior service missionaries for BYU-Pathway, and senior missionaries at BYU-Hawaii. They are cur-rently serving as missionaries in the Tahiti Papeete Mission where Russ served as a young man.